Preparing for a Wedding in the Episcopal Church

Tobias Stanislas Haller, BSG

Church Publishing
NEW YORK

Unless otherwise noted, the Scripture quotations contained herein are from the New Revised Standard Version Bible, copyright © 1989 by the Division of Christian Education of the National Council of Churches of Christ in the U.S.A. Used by permission. All rights reserved.

Church Publishing, 19 East 34th Street, New York, NY 10016
www.churchpublishing.org

Cover design by Laurie Klein Westhafer, Bounce Design
Typeset by Beth Oberholtzer Design

Library of Congress Cataloging-in-Publication Data

Names: Haller, Tobias Stanislas, author.
Title: Preparing for a wedding in the Episcopal Church / Tobias Stanislas Haller BSG.
Description: New York : Church Publishing, 2017. | Includes bibliographical references and index.
Identifiers: LCCN 2016029660 (print) | LCCN 2016038600 (ebook) | ISBN 9780819232670 (pbk.) | ISBN 9780819232687 (ebook)
Subjects: LCSH: Marriage—Religious aspects—Episcopal Church. | Marriage service. | Weddings—United States.
Classification: LCC BX5949.M3 H35 2017 (print) | LCC BX5949.M3 (ebook) | DDC 264/.03085—dc23
LC record available at https://lccn.loc.gov/2016029660

Printed in the United States of America

Contents

CONTENTS

Introduction

Marriage greets us with what seem to be limitless possibilities. It can also bring us up short as we confront finite limitations. Marriage has cosmic significance, but that significance is expressed by means of very earthly realities. The wedding itself serves as the pivotal moment in which the huge array of options comes face-to-face with the practical limits of what can and does take place. This moment is the start of what the couple intend to last for the rest of their lives; it is a single moment open to a wonderful range of future possibilities. Think of it as the narrow point on an hourglass—the possibilities of the past narrow down to that moment, which then allows new possible futures that could not come to be, were it not for that specific action of consent and commitment. As the old hymn put it, "Blessed be the tie that binds"—it is in accepting and committing to one's spouse, pruning away all other possibilities, that the marriage blooms into the reality it becomes, day by day. The wedding is a moment—the marriage is a life.

This booklet is intended as a guide to clergy, church musicians, and couples, to map out some of the possibilities available to them, and to offer counsel as to how best to make use of the time and treasure invested in planning and experiencing this pivotal event in the couple's life together.

First, however, a disclaimer: because marriage is governed by "both laws"—the liturgical and canon law of the church, and the civil law of the state (and in some places of the local jurisdiction as well)—and because these laws are not uniform across the whole of the church and the nation(s) in which the church functions, you are well advised to check with your local authority (sacred and secular) to find out what may be permissible or discouraged, or even mandated or forbidden, in your diocese and state (or city). Clergy in particular, due to the fact that they wear two hats as they exercise both the sacred and secular functions, are advised to be familiar with any requirements of their diocese and their civil jurisdiction.

With this in mind, some clergy have found it helpful to put some rules or guidelines in place in advance, in the form of a marriage policy statement, in order to limit the range of possibilities available. Couples will find this to be a help rather than a constraint, aiding them to focus on what is central to the event and what is peripheral—what is required, recommended, discouraged, or disallowed. This guide is intended to serve as a help in putting such a set of guidelines in place. An example form is offered in the last section, but it is intended only to serve as a starting point. It is open to as much amendment as the clergy and parish think best serves your situation, taking into account whatever local requirements may be in force.

The Marriage Canon: What the Church Requires

The Episcopal Church's marriage canon was extensively revised in 2015. This revision was intended to bring greater clarity to the responsibilities of the couple and the clergy, to restore a chronology that had been lost in earlier piecemeal revisions, and to bring the canon into conformity with the liturgical rites available since 1979. Because the canon is laid out in chronological order, it will serve as a framework for the following examination of the process that leads up to the wedding, and the wedding itself.

CANON I.18: Of the Celebration and Blessing of Marriage

Sec. 1. Every Member of the Clergy of this Church shall conform to the laws of the State governing the creation of the civil status of marriage, and also these canons concerning the solemnization of marriage. Members of the Clergy may solemnize a marriage using any of the liturgical forms authorized by this Church.

Sec. 2. The couple shall notify the Member of the Clergy of their intent to marry at least thirty days prior to the solemnization; Provided, that if one of the parties is a member of the Congregation of the Member of the Clergy, or both parties can furnish satisfactory evidence of the need for shortening the time, this requirement can be waived for weighty cause; in which case the Member of the Clergy shall immediately report this action in writing to the Bishop.

Sec. 3. Prior to the solemnization, the Member of the Clergy shall determine:

(a) that both parties have the right to marry according to the laws of the State and consent to do so freely, without fraud, coercion, mistake as to the identity of either, or mental reservation; and

(b) that at least one of the parties is baptized; and

(c) that both parties have been instructed by the Member of the Clergy, or a person known by the Member of the Clergy to be competent and responsible, in the nature, purpose, and meaning, as well as the rights, duties and responsibilities of marriage.

Sec. 4. Prior to the solemnization, the parties shall sign the following Declaration of Intention:

We understand the teaching of the church that God's purpose for our marriage is for our mutual joy, for the help and comfort we will give to each other in prosperity and adversity, and, when it is God's will, for the gift and heritage of children and their nurture in the knowledge and love of God. We also understand that our marriage is to be un-conditional, mutual, exclusive, faithful, and lifelong; and we engage to make the utmost effort to accept these gifts and fulfill these duties, with the help of God and the support of our community.

Sec. 5. At least two witnesses shall be present at the solemnization, and together with the Member of the Clergy and the parties, sign the record of the solemnization in the proper register; which record shall include the date and place of the solemnization, the names of the witnesses, the parties and their parents, the age of the parties, Church status, and residence(s).

Sec. 6. A bishop or priest may pronounce a blessing upon a civil marriage using any of the liturgical forms authorized by this Church.

Sec. 7. It shall be within the discretion of any Member of the Clergy of this Church to decline to solemnize or bless any marriage.[1]

[1] "Constitution and Canons of The Episcopal Church—2015," 58. Revisions adopted at the General Convention of The Episcopal Church, Salt Lake City, UT, June 25–July 3, 2015. Available online at www.generalconvention.org.

The Officiant

The Civil Law

Every Member of the Clergy of this Church shall conform to the laws of the State governing the creation of the civil status of marriage . . . (Canon I.18.1)

It is beyond the scope of this resource to include information that would cover all of the civil jurisdictions in which the Episcopal Church (TEC) functions, a number of them outside the United States. This is due to the very wide range of civil requirements as they are applied in different states and municipalities both in the United States and in those other parts of the world in which TEC has a diocesan, parochial, or mission presence. Some of these regulations concern the couple; these include age requirements, need for parental consent, degree of kinship within which marriage is permitted, and status of previous marriages. Other regulations concern who may serve as an authorized officiant. Clergy are well advised to familiarize themselves with the civil law in their own town, city, state, and in some cases country, to be sure that both they and the couple are in full compliance with the civil law.

In general, most jurisdictions require that couples obtain a marriage license or other form of registration prior to the solemnization of their marriage. Such licenses are usually applicable for a set period of time, for example sixty days from the date of registration, so it is important that the couple not obtain the license too far in advance of the wedding, or—in places where a waiting period is required for a license—too late. The license serves as a summary of the civil requirements, in that one must be in compliance in order to obtain the license; clergy and the couple can take some assurance that the license certifies the couple have a legal right to marry.

When it comes to the officiant, some jurisdictions require all marriage officiants to register with the local civil authority, while others consider being an ordained minister in any religious body to be adequate without further registration. Clergy should check on the local policy soon after beginning ministry in a new area, in order to be prepared for the first marriage request that may come along.

A Note on Terminology
ABOUT THE OFFICIANT

Various rites refer to the officiant by different terms: *celebrant*, *officiant*, and in the newer liturgies, *presider*. Some civil jurisdictions use the term *solemnizer*. Whatever term is used for the officiant, it is good to remember that in the church's view the actual ministers of the marriage are the couple themselves—they administer marriage to each other. The officiant is there almost in the capacity of a master of ceremonies, or the conductor of an orchestra, overseeing the flow of the rite, and of course making specific contributions to it. But the heart of marriage is the couple, not the clergy.

The Church's Law

Every Member of the Clergy of this Church shall conform to . . . these canons concerning the solemnization of marriage. (Canon I.18.1)

The canons of the church lay out the responsibilities and rights of the clergy, and these will be examined at greater length in each of the following sections. The Book of Common Prayer (BCP), which is the liturgical law of the Episcopal Church, also spells out many of the possibilities and limitations.

In the Episcopal Church the ordinary officiant at a wedding is a priest (or a bishop). This is so because "such ministers alone have the function of pronouncing the nuptial blessing, and of celebrating the Holy Eucharist" (BCP 422). In some jurisdictions a deacon may solemnize a marriage under the civil law. The church places some limitations on how a deacon may do so, if at all permitted by the local church policy. Moreover, the rubrics (prayer book instructions) state that a deacon (where civil law allows) should officiate only when "no priest or bishop is available"; when officiating, a deacon must omit the nuptial blessing. (It should be noted that this blessing is one of the two chief functions of a church wedding—the other being witness and support. The absence of a blessing does not invalidate or otherwise alter the nature of the marriage itself, since the actual *ministers* of marriage are the couple. But the nuptial blessing is a central element of the rite.)

A deacon may participate fully in a marriage in which a priest or bishop is officiating, and "may deliver the charge, ask for the Declaration of Consent, read the Gospel . . ." and assist in the regular diaconal functions when the Eucharist follows. An assisting priest may also take on such tasks as arranged by the clergy in charge. In a large parish, it is not unusual for a couple who are active members to want to involve all of the clergy who minister there, and the rubric provides for just such a possibility.

9

The Choice of Liturgy

. . . Members of the Clergy may solemnize a marriage using any of the liturgical forms authorized by this Church. (Canon I.18.1)

The Book of Common Prayer offers a primary liturgy entitled "The Celebration and Blessing of a Marriage" (page 423). (Henceforth referred to as CBM.) This rite includes many options, as well as a few specific requirements. The BCP also includes a supplementary "Order for Marriage" (page 435) (OM) that opens options even more broadly, providing an outline of actions that must be included, but without providing an explicit text for anything other than the marriage vows. This virtual *carte blanche* concerning language is so open to adaptation that one might, for example, make use of most of the 1662 Book of Common Prayer marriage liturgy. It is beyond the scope of this booklet to include all of the options and possibilities, but many will be outlined in what follows. (Also not addressed in this document is the BCP liturgy for "The Blessing of a Civil Marriage" on page 433. This is just what the title indicates, and is available for couples who for whatever reason marry civilly and then wish to have their marriage blessed. This liturgy is very flexible, and can be adapted so as to resemble the marriage liturgy. Most of what is said below in the section on liturgical options applies.)

In addition to the Book of Common Prayer, the 2015 General Convention provided for the use of three additional liturgies, with some restrictions. These were presented as part of the Standing Commission on Liturgy and Music proposal contained in "Liturgical Resources I: I Will Bless You and You Will Be a Blessing, Revised and Expanded 2015," as amended by the General Convention. The three liturgies are:

❖ "The Witnessing and Blessing of a Lifelong Covenant" (henceforth WBLC)

❖ "The Witnessing and Blessing of a Marriage" (WBM)

❖ "The Celebration and Blessing of a Marriage 2" (CBM2)

The first of these (WBLC) is not a marriage in a legal sense (under either church or civil law). It was and is intended for the blessing of a couple who intend a common life but who are unable to marry legally. At the time of its proposal it was intended primarily for same-sex couples who lived in states (or nations) that had not adopted marriage equality. The situation in the fifty states changed during the 2015 General Convention session, but there remain nondomestic jurisdictions of the Episcopal Church where same-sex couples, as of this writing, cannot wed under civil law, and this liturgy is available for their use, with the authorization of the diocesan authority. As this liturgy is not technically a marriage, it will not be given expanded attention in this volume.

The second rite (WBM) is a revised marriage liturgy that follows the form and structure of WBLC, and in circumstances where the use of WBLC is contemplated, much of what is said about WBM may apply. This rite differs from the BCP marriage liturgy in structure and language. For one thing, it follows the basic structure of other pastoral rites such as Baptism, Confirmation, and Ordination, in which exhortation, presentation, reflection on Scripture, and prayer *precede* the central action of the rite. (In the BCP, liturgy prayers for the couple *follow* the exchange of vows and declaration of marriage; some have experienced this placement, introduced in the 1979 liturgy, as an interruption to the flow of the liturgical drama.) The rite is *shaped* more like the other pastoral rites, and it shares aspects familiar from the Eucharist, such as the opening acclamation. Furthermore, it is intended that the Eucharist be a normative part of the celebration (though the rubrics indicate it remains optional). This rite is also explicitly suited to use on a Sunday as the main worship of the church, which is particularly appropriate if one or both of the couple are active members of the congregation. Finally, though WBM was originally conceived for same-sex couples, many mixed-sex couples have found that they prefer this liturgy for a number of reasons related to both form and language.

The third rite (CBM2) is a modest revision of the BCP marriage liturgy, following it in form, and with minor changes in the language to make it suitable for any couple. The two 2015 rites, and that of the 1979 BCP, will be the primary liturgical focus of this booklet. Both of the new marriage rites were adopted under the Episcopal Church's constitutional provision for trial use leading to possible inclusion in the Book of Common Prayer, and as such are to be available to any couple, under the direction and with the permission of the diocesan bishop.

This is where the phrase in Canon I.18, "authorized by this Church," is important. The Book of Common Prayer is, of course, authorized for use throughout the church and no further permission is needed for its use (though in the case of remarriage after divorce, clergy are required to get permission from the diocesan authority).

The additional rites being offered under trial use are subject to the direction and permission of the bishop or diocesan authority. Clergy should familiarize themselves with the policy in place in their diocese.

Couples and clergy will make the decision as to which rite to use, and the choice of options possible within each rite, as part of their conversation and counseling.

A Note on Terminology
ABOUT ATTENDANTS

Because of the many changes in marriage over the years, some terminology that might seem quaint in other contexts (or have an entirely different meaning) has remained in use. (Even most hotels no longer refer to "maids" but to "housekeeping.") We've come far since Downton Abbey, but we still have maids and matrons of honor in many a wedding.

However, we have also seen the appearance of new terms arising to meet new occasions; the best man may be a best woman, and a man of honor may proudly take his place in the procession. There is no reason that a little girl can't carry rings or a little boy can't carry flowers. Rather than attempt to force a form of consistency on this variety, this booklet will trust to the readers' understanding to make the adjustments needed for their own circumstances.

On Whether to Have the Eucharist

Whether to include the Eucharist as part of the wedding is a decision best reached with some care. In some situations (for example, an inter-faith or mixed marriage) it is probably best not to include Holy Communion, as one of the couple may not be able to participate fully. The makeup of the assembly is also a factor: are the couple's friends and family likely to partici-pate? If not, it may seem odd, and not a little

contrary to the concept of "communion," if only the couple and a few of the immediate atten-dants receive. Obviously, this need not be an issue when the couple are active members of the congregation, along with many of the guests. Fortunately, all of the authorized wedding rites make provision for including or omitting Holy Communion.

An Outline of Wedding Possibilities

The chart on the next page shows in outline the structure of these two types of liturgy (CBM and CBM2 having the same structure, with minimal change in language). Optional elements in each are in square brackets. As you can see, the main difference between the two types of liturgy concerns the sequence in which

certain events happen: reflection on Scripture in the ministry of the Word precedes or fol-lows the presentation and the declaration of consent (which are themselves in a different order depending on the rite); and the prayers for the couple come before or after the exchange of vows.

A Note on Place

At the time appointed, the persons to be married, with their witnesses, assemble in the church or some other appropriate place. (BCP 423)

Although many couples—perhaps most—wish to be married in the church building, some couples may wish to celebrate their marriage in another place: a botanical garden, by the seashore, or even in a space dedicated to that purpose in the venue chosen for the wedding reception. This resource will focus on wed-dings that take place in the church building, but much of what is said here can be adapted to other settings. Marriage in the church is a

powerful symbol for a couple who are active members of a congregation, and may be more convenient for other congregation members. A marriage celebrated in another setting will necessarily lack that "note," but may, with care, maintain the "melody." A marriage in church can be an evangelistic opportunity even when few of the friends and family members have any church connection.

Celebration and Blessing of a Marriage (BCP & 2)	Witnessing and Blessing of a Marriage
[Music for the entrance]	[Music for the entrance]
Opening Exhortation	Opening Greeting and Exhortation
The Declaration of Consent	
[Presentation or giving in marriage]	
Collect	Collect of the Day
Scripture Reading(s) [followed by a psalm, hymn, or anthem] [ending with a Gospel reading if communion is to follow]	Scripture Reading(s) [followed by a psalm, hymn, or anthem] [ending with a Gospel reading if communion is to follow]
[Homily]	Sermon
	[Presentation in marriage]
	The Declaration of Consent
	Prayers for the couple and community
	[The Lord's Prayer (unless Eucharist follows)]
The Exchange of Vows	The Exchange of Vows
[Blessing of Ring(s)]	[Blessing of Ring(s)]
Exchange of Ring(s)	[Exchange of Ring(s) (if rings were exchanged previously, they may be blessed on the couple's hands)]
Joining of hands and pronouncement of marriage	Joining of hands and pronouncement of marriage
[The Lord's Prayer (unless Eucharist follows)]	
Prayers for the Couple	
Blessing of the Marriage	Blessing of the Couple
[The Peace] (and the couple's mutual greeting)	The Peace (including the couple's mutual greeting)
	Blessing of the People and dismissal, unless communion follows
Departure of the wedding party, unless communion follows	Departure of the wedding party, unless communion follows

And So It Begins . . .

The couple shall notify the Member of the Clergy of their intent to marry at least thirty days prior to the solemnization; Provided, that if one of the parties is a member of the Congregation of the Member of the Clergy, or both parties can furnish satisfactory evidence of the need for shortening the time, this requirement can be waived for weighty cause; in which case the Member of the Clergy shall immediately report this action in writing to the Bishop. (Canon I.18.2)

It is not unusual for clergy—especially if they serve a picturesque church—to receive unsolicited calls beginning, "I want to get married in your church" from people with little or no connection to the congregation, often having already chosen a date a few weeks away and having hired a hall for the reception. This is an extreme example, and is offset by the welcome call from members of the congregation that they hope to be married in the church later that year. The canon gives the clergy an easy escape from the former, and the ability to celebrate the latter, by requiring at least thirty days notice prior to the intended date of the wedding. The provision to shorten the time is available when at least one of the couple is a parishioner, or both can provide a good reason for such an abbreviation. Such situations are not unusual in wartime, when one of the couple is about to be mobilized for service; employment transfers can result in such a necessity as well. Similar weighty causes are subject to the judgment of the clergy, and when granted, such "shortening of the time" is to be reported to the bishop.

At the time of first contact, particularly with couples not connected with the congregation, it is helpful to have a copy of guidelines and policies available, laying out whatever requirements the congregation might have. (Members of the congregation may have advance knowledge of these policies and already be prepared to abide by them.) A sample form is provided in the appendix, and you should feel free to amend it to suit your situation.

Timing is, of course, important—not merely to be sure the clergy (and the church) are available on the day the couple wish to wed, but to provide time for other requirements, such as premarital instruction. In the case of remarriage after a divorce or annulment, the clergy will need additional time to review the paperwork and submit a report and request for judgment to the bishop.

Eligibility to Marry

The Civil Side

Prior to the solemnization, the Member of the Clergy shall determine . . . that both parties have the right to marry according to the laws of the State and consent to do so freely, without fraud, coercion, mistake as to the identity of either, or mental reservation . . . (Canon I.18.3.a)

In many jurisdictions, clergy have the assistance of the civil authorities in carrying out the responsibility of determining that the couple have the right to marry, as they will have to demonstrate this in order to obtain a marriage license. States have many requirements that need not concern the clergy beyond being sure they have been met. These include limits or requirements concerning age, parental notice or permission, health certification, and degree of kin relationship (if any). Clergy are advised to familiarize themselves with the local law so as to advise couples prior to obtaining a license if anything in their relationship might cause delay or even prevent their being married.

The requirements of free consent and lack of fraud, coercion, mistaken identity, or mental reservation ensure that the marriage will be valid. The lack of free consent, or use of fraud or force, for example, would constitute grounds to nullify the marriage in a civil context. These impediments would also have impact on the church's view of the validity of the marriage, and would be grounds for annulment, a declaration that no marriage actually took place.

One of the obvious requirements of the civil law is that a person seeking to marry cannot be married to another person still living. The state recognizes the termination of marriage through divorce; the church has its own procedure for reviewing such terminations of marriage and authorizing the remarriage of a person who has been divorced. This process is laid out in Canon I.19.2–3

> Sec. 2 (a) Any member of this Church whose marriage has been annulled or dissolved by a civil court may apply to the Bishop or Ecclesiastical Authority of the Diocese in which such person is legally or canonically resident for a judgment as to his or her marital status in the eyes of the Church. Such judgment may be a recognition of the nullity, or of the termination of the said marriage; Provided, that no such judgment shall be construed as affecting in any way the legitimacy of children or the civil validity of the former relationship.

> (b) Every judgment rendered under this Section shall be in writing and shall be made a matter of permanent record in the Archives of the Diocese.

> Sec. 3. No Member of the Clergy of this Church shall solemnize the marriage of any person who has been the husband or wife of any other person then living, nor shall any member of this Church enter into a marriage when either of the contracting parties has been the husband or the wife of any other person then living, except as hereinafter provided:

(a) The Member of the Clergy shall be satisfied by appropriate evidence that the prior marriage has been annulled or dissolved by a final judgment or decree of a civil court of competent jurisdiction.

(b) The Member of the Clergy shall have instructed the parties that continuing concern must be shown for the well being of the former spouse, and of any children of the prior marriage.

(c) The Member of the Clergy shall consult with and obtain the consent of the Bishop of the Diocese wherein the Member of the Clergy is canonically resident or the Bishop of the Diocese in which the Member of the Clergy is licensed to officiate prior to, and shall report to that Bishop, the solemnization of any marriage under this Section.

(d) If the proposed marriage is to be solemnized in a jurisdiction other than the one in which the consent has been given, the consent shall be affirmed by the Bishop of that jurisdiction.[1]

Clergy are advised to be familiar with their own bishop's policy and requirements in this regard. Some bishops will rely almost entirely on the clergy review of the "evidence that the prior marriage has been annulled or dissolved" (I.19.3.a) and the clergy recommendation, but other bishops may wish to examine the documentation personally, and may have set time limits in place in order to fit their schedule. Clergy will be wise to be familiar with these limits in order to advise couples (one or both of whom may be in this situation) of any additional time needed prior to their marriage being solemnized, which could be weeks or months.

The Sacred Side

Prior to the solemnization, the Member of the Clergy shall determine . . . that at least one of the parties is baptized . . . (Canon I.18.3.a)

In addition to the other requirements, which are shared with almost all civil jurisdictions, the church adds one additional requirement: that at least one of the couple be baptized. Baptism in the Episcopal Church is not required, as this church recognizes baptism as a universal Christian rite. Nor does the church's law require that either of the couple be active members in the Episcopal Church or any other church. It is, of course, within the discretion of the clergy and the congregation to have more stringent requirements in place, in accord with Section 7 of the Canon (see page 24, "When Not to Wed"). They may, for example, wish only to celebrate marriages when at least one of the couple is a member of the congregation. Such policies need to be weighed against the possibility that marriages might have for exposing un- or dischurched people to the church, at a happier occasion and (one hopes) long prior to the other main exposure such people experience: the funeral of a friend or loved one.

---

[1] "Constitution and Canons of The Episcopal Church—2015," 59–60.

The Episcopal Church thus *allows* for marriage in which one of the couple is non-Christian. This could be an agnostic or an adherent of a different faith tradition. If the non-Christian party is observant in their own tradition, the use of the BCP Order for Marriage may provide for the greatest flexibility to allow participation by clergy or leaders of that faith community. It will also be important for clergy and the couple to address the role of the couple's faith in their life together, and the extent to which this might generate tensions or difficulties. Since the marriage liturgies highlight the role of marriage in the gift and heritage of children, concern for the religious tradition (if any) in which children will be raised is also important. It is good as well to consider the impact being married to a Christian might have on the non-Christian's participation in their own religious body, and vice versa. Such concerns will need to be on the table early in the process, to avoid possible misunderstanding or disappointed expectations. Needless to say, in an interfaith marriage ceremony the Eucharist would not be celebrated, since one of the couple could not participate fully.

More commonly, one of the couple may be a Christian but from another church. This can also be a source of tension and difficulty, and the concern for children is the same, as is the possibility of impact on the couple's individual church life. Marriage between an Episcopalian and a Roman Catholic raises particular issues. Generally speaking, a Roman Catholic is not permitted to marry a person who is not also a Roman Catholic unless they have received a dispensation allowing the marriage. This only creates a difficulty for the Roman Catholic spouse if they wish to remain active in the Roman Catholic Church—which will not recognize them as being married under Roman church law. (There is a procedure for "regularizing" such situations.) Should this situation apply, the Roman Catholic spouse should have a serious conversation with their own pastor, to be sure this will not create difficulties. In many areas clergy from various traditions know each other and meet for ecumenical fellowship, and in such cases they may already have local or regional policies in place to ease any tensions such a situation might create. Episcopal clergy are advised to familiarize themselves with the local policies on interfaith marriages, and on Episcopal/Roman Catholic marriages in particular.

Some sensitivity will also have to be shown about whether to include the Eucharist as part of a marriage ceremony in which one of the couple comes from a Christian tradition that would not approve of their receiving Holy Communion in the Episcopal Church. The makeup of the assembly in such a case should also be kept in mind.

Premarital Instruction

Prior to the solemnization, the Member of the Clergy shall determine . . . that both parties have been instructed by the Member of the Clergy, or a person known by the Member of the Clergy to be competent and responsible, in the nature, purpose, and meaning, as well as the rights, duties and responsibilities of marriage . . . (Canon I.18.3.c)

Prior to the solemnization, the parties shall sign the following Declaration of Intention:

We understand the teaching of the church that God's purpose for our marriage is for our mutual joy, for the help and comfort we will give to each other in prosperity and adversity, and, when it is God's will, for the gift and heritage of children and their nurture in the knowledge and love of God. We also understand that our marriage is to be unconditional, mutual, exclusive, faithful, and lifelong; and we engage to make the utmost effort to accept these gifts and fulfill these duties, with the help of God and the support of our community. (Canon I.18.4)

Clergy are required either to instruct the couple in preparation for their marriage or determine that a competent and responsible person has provided such instruction. A large parish may be fortunate in having more than one clergy member who specializes in this area of pastoral ministry, or a lay leader with professional skill as a marriage counselor; however, in most situations this task falls to the member of the clergy in charge of the congregation.

The canon very briefly summarizes the content of the instruction, and the Declaration of Intention was specifically designed (in the 2015 revision of the canon) to provide a modest fleshing out of that summary. At the very least it can serve as an outline for conversation with a couple at their first meeting with the cleric.

The extent of the clergy responsibility, the cleric's own skills, and the expectation of the couple should be kept in mind. The actual clergy responsibility is limited to what the canon lays out—that is, that the couple understand certain things about marriage. Clergy are not expected, or required, to be full-fledged marriage counselors, and may not have the skills for that kind of work. They should also be ready, should they discern any serious problems they do not feel themselves able to address, to refer any couple to a professional counselor or therapist.

In consultation with the couple, the clergy may limit the instruction to the canonical requirements; they may choose to supplement this with a minimal or extensive *compatibility inventory* or *checklist* for the couple, similar to that employed by many dating services; or they may choose a more fully developed program along the lines of the "Pre-Cana" instruction used in some churches.

In any case, the course of instruction will necessarily vary depending on the skills of the clergy, and the age and situation of the couple. A young couple in their twenties will want to address their future married life differently than a couple in their sixties with grown children from a previous marriage. Same-sex couples may have particular concerns that mixed-sex couples will not need to address. Fortunately there is a very wide range of marriage preparation material available—some of it broadly adaptable to many circumstances, some tailored to particular needs. It is beyond the scope of this booklet to provide an exhaustive list, but following are a few of the available resources, with notes on their particular use.

The clergy, working with the couple, will make the ultimate decision on the form the instruction takes. Some clergy will take a seat-of-the-pants approach and forgo the use of any set format; others may find a particular form with which they are comfortable. In any case, it is good to have a general note on the subject of premarital instruction as part of the guidelines available to couples interested in marriage. Because requirements vary from place to place (and tradition to tradition), couples may be expecting more, or less, time to be spent in this process.

Here are a few of the available resources for premarital instruction. (Adapted from the report of the Standing Commission on Liturgy and Music to the 2015 General Convention, based on a 2010 survey. New resources are always being introduced; be aware that many are geared to a narrow constituency, and not all will be suitable for a given couple or situation.)

Prepare/Enrich
(Life Innovations Inc.)
https://www.prepare-enrich.com

This is a widely used assessment tool that addresses a comprehensive range of issues and concerns a couple might or will face. Using it requires some training for the clergy or lay leader, who is called a *facilitator*. Many are comfortable knowing that there is additional support for the instructor as well as the couple. It is an internet-based system, so computer access will be necessary.

Premarriage Awareness Inventory
(Logos Productions)
http://www.logosproductions.com/content/marriage-preparation

This is a popular inventory format, with the advantage of three different inventories designed for three common situations: couples who have not lived together and are marrying for the first time; couples with one or both previously married; and couples who have been living together for some time prior to the intended marriage. Logos also offers *A Good Beginning*, a short book for couples that may be useful in raising issues and concerns for discussion with each other and the clergy.

The Marriage Journey: Preparation and Provisions for Life Together
Linda Grenz and Delbert Glover
(Church Publishing, 2003)
https://www.churchpublishing.org/products/themarriagejourney

This resource comes from the Episcopal Church, and is therefore well suited for Episcopal clergy and couples. It doesn't include an inventory mechanism, but provides for conversation and exploration of all of the concerns couples will have and experience. You might make use of it in conjunction with one of the inventories listed above. This resource is well suited to couples who already are living together or who have children as part of their current household.

Don't Forget to Sign

The last instruction session would be a good time to have the couple sign the required Declaration of Intention. This document should be retained by the cleric in a file with all marriage information. A sample form is provided at the end of this booklet, supplemented by language to assure that all requirements in addition to those spelled out in the canon have been met. It is also possible to create a simple version of just the Declaration, suitable for framing, to be presented to the couple, with a copy retained in the church files.

Witnessing and Registration

At least two witnesses shall be present at the solemnization, and together with the Member of the Clergy and the parties, sign the record of the solemnization in the proper register; which record shall include the date and place of the solemnization, the names of the witnesses, the parties and their parents, the age of the parties, Church status, and residence(s). (Canon I.18.5)

A principal function of the church with regard to marriage has long been its testimony to the fact that a couple are married. Clandestine or secret marriages were outlawed long ago, and the public nature of marriage has been a major feature of the rite. This has included such customs as the publication of banns of marriage—a formal notice to the community that a couple intend to marry. In the earliest period, the celebration of at least the first part of the wedding took place on the steps of the church porch rather than within the church itself. In the days before the development of means by which the public could be well informed, such provisions helped to ensure some of the key factors of eligibility: identity and marital independence. In a village culture such public notice was one way to be sure that the spouses were who they claimed to be, and that neither had a living spouse in the next town over. There is a relic of these principles in the opening call to the congregation for any objections to the marriage taking place.

Such objections are, thankfully, rare, but the church is still an important witness to the marriage, and is a registrar of the fact the marriage has taken place. Clergy, in addition to whatever civil requirements exist with regard to the marriage license, are required to provide the couple, their witnesses, and themselves a "proper register" to record the relevant information concerning the marriage, and the signatures of the participants.

Long-standing custom has this signing take place in the sacristy or vestry meeting room at some point immediately after the liturgy. However, in many places the couple and their witnesses may be at greater pains to have photographs taken or to depart for the reception. Some clergy and couples have found it more convenient—and more meaningful—to make the signing of the register (and the license, if required) part of the liturgy. In addition to the convenience, this raises the signing to a ceremonial level and enhances the solemnity of the act. As with the signing of the Oath of Conformity in the ordination rites (by one about to be ordained a deacon, priest, or bishop), this very public act helps to emphasize and celebrate the responsibilities undertaken and the new life commenced, and provides an additional visible opportunity for participation by the witnesses. (The clergy, of course, can sign the register and fill in other information after the celebration. They are well advised to obtain the names and addresses of the witnesses in advance of the celebration, as reading handwritten signatures can be a challenge.) If a spouse takes a new married name, this will be the first time they sign with it—so celebrating this as a public act serves to enhance that unique moment. (An additional tip: color-coded Post-it arrow-flags can be a help in guiding the signatories to the right line in the register and on the license.)

21

If clergy and couples choose to sign the register in this public way, the placement of the book will depend on the space. Some have the book conveniently placed near the altar on a small table, on the altar itself, or on a lectern. It may be ideal to use the latter, placed so that the signers are facing the assembly. Since much of the marriage liturgy involves the couple either facing each other or away from the assembly, this opportunity for their faces and actions to be visible is a significant enhancement.

For Those Already Married

A bishop or priest may pronounce a blessing upon a civil marriage using any of the liturgical forms authorized by this Church. (Canon I.18.6)

The Book of Common Prayer provides a liturgy for the blessing of a civil marriage, which may be used in situations where the couple has already married under civil law. (The civil law in some countries does not grant clergy the authority to solemnize marriages. In France, for example, it is common for a couple to wed in the town hall and then process to the church.)

In addition to the BCP rite, the new Witnessing and Blessing of a Marriage may be used by couples who have already married civilly, or who have made some other form of lifelong commitment that is not recognized as a civil marriage; since the cleric exercises both an ecclesiastical and a civil function, this ceremony bestows the church's blessing on a civil marriage, and regularizes a couple's existing relationship *as* a civil marriage. This recognizes the long-standing theological position that the ministers of marriage are the couple, even though the civil authority in most places requires licensing and solemnization. This rite also provides that if the couple "have previously given and worn rings as a symbol of their commitment, the rings may be blessed on the hands of the couple."

When Not to Wed

It shall be within the discretion of any Member of the Clergy of this Church to decline to solemnize or bless any marriage. (Canon I.18.7)

The last clause of the marriage canon provides clergy with the discretion to decline to take part in any particular solemnization or blessing of a marriage. This principle may be applied in cases of conscientious objection or in cases where the clergy are not satisfied the couple are prepared to undertake and fulfill the responsibilities of marriage. This provision first came into the canon about the time when the church instituted a procedure for the marriage of persons divorced from a still-living spouse, to which some bishops and clergy objected.

There are a number of circumstances that could justify clergy declining to participate, but it is important to note that the clergy do not have to explain their reasons. However, if the reason is based on a permanent impediment—such as a wish to marry for some reason other than, or in contradiction to, the purposes of marriage recognized by the church—it would be fitting for the cleric to explain why they declined. For example, a couple who say they are marrying so as to hasten one of the parties' citizenship acceptance, and that they intend to file for divorce soon after, should likely be told that the church would not recognize such a marriage as valid, due to the impediment of *defective intent*. (One cannot make the marriage vows with one's fingers crossed! The revised Declaration of Intention in Canon I.18 spells out the grounds for a finding of defective intent. Clergy not only may, but should, decline to solemnize a marriage in such cases.)

If the reason the clergy wish to decline to solemnize has to do with some defect that could be or will be remedied with time—for example, a couple who have only known each other for a very short time—it would be appropriate for the clergy to tell them to return at a later date, after they have come to know each other better.

Of course, another reason to decline would be the inability of the clergy or the couple to comply with the requirements of the church or civil law—if, for example, neither of the couple is baptized. (This might be an opportunity to commend baptismal instruction and the catechumenate.) One of the difficulties noted at the outset is the tendency of some couples to fix the date of their wedding (and the wedding reception) prior to contacting the church, not realizing that time is required for preparation or, in the case of a divorced party, for approval by the bishop.

As the liturgy itself says, marriage is not to be entered into lightly or hastily—and that goes for the clergy as well as the couple.

Planning the Liturgy

Clergy and their parishes are advised to have policies or guidelines in place concerning weddings, to address the expectations couples may have concerning what will take place, and when and how. Much depends on the circumstances of the church itself: how large is it; what is the layout of the nave, choir, and sanctuary; is there a parking lot or driveway; is there a space that could be used for a reception; and so on. The following is a guide laying out some of the possibilities, which a parish is wise to prune down to a listing that fits its own capacities and needs.

The sample forms provided at the end of this booklet are based on the customary developed for a particular parish, based on its limitations and capacities. Your church will have its own strong points that lend it to weddings, or it may have aspects that create difficulties in providing what a couple wish to do. The old saying, "Reality is our friend," is good to keep in mind. But it is also good to have a written policy or customary so as to dissuade unwanted features and rule out the impossible. Establishing a set of policy guidelines, with provision for exceptions, is a wise exercise in prudence.

When and Where?

Saturdays are traditional wedding days for many couples, and late morning or early afternoon seems to be the most practical time. The new liturgy for the Witnessing and Blessing of a Marriage is designed to allow its use on a Sunday, which may be particularly appropriate if one or both of the couple are active members of the congregation. It is, of course, possible to plan weddings to take place at any time that is convenient for all concerned, and this is sometimes a considerable balancing act for the couple, attendants, family and friends, and the clergy and church musician(s).

Couples should be advised to include the actual time of the wedding on the wedding invitation; some have developed a bad habit of putting a time that is earlier than the actual time to accommodate the chronically late—but this is both confusing and discourteous to those who arrive in a timely fashion. It is essential that the couple provide the clergy with a copy of any wedding invitation, to avoid any such confusion about date, time, and place. Upon receiving such a copy, it is helpful for the clergy to remind the couple about the importance of punctuality—both as a courtesy to the guests and out of respect for the clergy and church musicians.

We noted above that the location for the wedding (usually the church) is expected to be "appropriate"—but that can be a subjective term. Practicality for all concerned is a major factor. If the Eucharist is to be part of the celebration, the church is likely the best place.

Big or Small? The Cast of Characters

A wedding with just the couple, their witnesses, and the clergy will require far less effort than a grand ceremony with multiple bridesmaids and groomsmen, instrumentalists in addition to the organist, and a large collection of family members. A wedding involving longtime members of the congregation will also differ from one celebrated for relative newcomers, or even strangers to the church. It is within the authority of clergy to decline to "take weddings" for those with no parish association. On the other hand, some churches (particularly those with beautiful architecture) may find themselves often called upon to celebrate just such marriages. This can be an opportunity to reach unchurched (or dischurched) people—beyond the couple themselves. It can also be a headache and a significant strain on clergy time and patience.

Layout of the Church: Inside

Weddings will have a different form if the church is a long rectangle (the "airplane" model) or is more open and "in the round." Is there a choir area between the nave and the sanctuary? Are there steps from the floor of the nave to the choir or altar? There is an old saying among church musicians that "the room always wins," and that is surely true for weddings. The "traditional wedding" outline in the appendix supposes a church with a central aisle, steps from the nave to the choir, and additional steps to the altar. Naturally a church will have discovered, or will discover, what works best in its "own room."

It is traditional for the exchange of vows and the prayers and blessings to take place at or near the altar rail (if there is one). Given the church's architecture, this may not be the most visible or desirable location. The use of a "wedding prie-dieu" (a double-wide kneeler for two with an arm/book-rest) in a convenient and perhaps more visible location, such as the center of the choir area, may be more appropriate.

One feature to plan for, in a traditional wedding, is a place for the groom to be situated with the clergy prior to the beginning of the rite. The sacristy often serves this purpose, but a vestry room or other space should be available. It is also wise to have a place for various attendants in the wedding party to gather away from the nave, preferably in the order in which they will enter.

In some churches it is customary to have friends and family of the couple sit on different sides of the church. This should match where the couple themselves will stand with their attendants. In the "traditional wedding" outline the bride is to the left (as one faces the altar) and the groom to the right; their friends and family are similarly situated in the congregational seating area.

Layout of the Church Grounds

Again, each church will have its own issues to address with regard to the outdoor situation. Is there parking available? If so, will people be alerted to be sure to leave room for the arrival—and egress for the departure—of the wedding party; in particular, where customary, to accommodate a bride's slightly delayed arrival. (More on how much of a delay is acceptable, and how to avoid it, will be addressed on page 32.) The issue may be how to allow a limo easy access if there are other cars blocking the way.

If the church grounds have open or garden space, it is customary to make it available for photographs or outdoor receptions, weather permitting.

Flowers and Decor

Flowers at weddings can range from a bouquet and boutonniere to large displays and hanging ropes, with bows and candles at all the pew-ends. One major issue to settle concerns when the flowers and other decor will arrive at the church (and who will be there to receive them), and how and when (and by whom) they will be set up. This is an important consideration in a busy church, as there may well be other liturgies scheduled. It is sometimes wise to plan the decorating immediately to precede the wedding rehearsal, as some of the same cast of characters will be involved.

There are a number of items that are particularly associated with weddings:

❖ The **aisle runner** is a (usually white) cloth or paper roll that is unfurled to cover the center aisle of the church prior to all or part of the opening entrance. (This is usually best handled by two ushers at either end of the roll.) The runner can be unrolled prior to the entry of the wedding party, prior to the flower bearer, or saved to be unrolled just for the bride (or both of the future spouses if they enter together).

❖ The **wedding prie-dieu** is a kneeler with shelf or armrest wide enough for the couple to kneel side by side. It can be used for the nuptial blessing if the couple choose not to be at the altar rail (or if there is none).

❖ Optionally, special **wedding cushions** can sometimes be used instead of the regular kneelers.

Wedding Planners

Wedding planners can be a blessing or a curse. They may have very fixed ideas as to how the ceremony should proceed that bear little resemblance to the requirements of the church's liturgy. They can be a boon in dealing with many of the aspects of the celebration, however, including taking charge of decor and flowers, and coordinating arrival times. A wise cleric will provide the wedding planner with a copy of the church customary or policies and go over it with them. The division of labor can be a help, so long as it is clear who is ultimately responsible for the conduct of the ceremony, which is to say, the clergy.

Photography

In an era in which it seems virtually everyone has a camera in their purse or pocket, as part of their smartphone, weddings have come to resemble press conferences. A parish may try to enforce a "no photography" policy, but human nature being what it is, it will be the rare wedding that is not recorded in the web-based cloud.

Some control can be exercised over professional photographers whom the couple may engage. This can range from a rule of "no photography during the celebration" to a concession allowing a professional photographer (or videographer) to be in a specific location or set of locations. It is helpful to remind couples that if they want their wedding to look like a wedding, it is best to have the photography staged after the celebration rather than during it.

With that in mind, clergy can offer the couple as much time as needed after the celebration to pose or recreate particular moments from the liturgy. This will be considerably less stressful for all concerned, as well as likely producing photographs that are superior in quality.

Music

Couples may expect that music will simply be a natural accompaniment to weddings that doesn't involve an actual person or persons. It is important at an early date to be sure that the parish musician(s) are available for the wedding. Music directors and organists normally have a "right of first refusal" for weddings—as weddings are often a part of a musician's livelihood. A talented organist may play at several churches, and so availability should be determined early on, as well as a standard fee. Again, such a fee would depend on the complexity of the liturgy, and that is for the organist to work out with the couple. If the couple want additional musicians, that too should be coordinated by the parish musical staff. It is not unusual to commission the organist to be present to provide a prelude prior to the actual wedding, as well as entrance music for the wedding party, and for the close. All of this should be worked out with care, and the fee discussed in detail. (As with the signing of the register being best placed within the context of the ceremony, it is also wise for someone to see to it that the musician(s) fee(s) are deposited prior to the celebration, as there is often considerable coming and going at the end.)

When it comes to musical selections, there are a number of "traditional" pieces of music associated with weddings, though the popularity of Wagner's *Lohengrin* and Mendelssohn's *Midsummer's Night's Dream* have diminished with time, and even Purcell's *Trumpet Tune* and Pachelbel's *Canon* may be less common. All of these are, of course, secular compositions that found a church home, and they may serve well, or even be the first choices. Some couples may wish to make use of other secular music, and this should be carefully worked through with the clergy and music director or organist. Song texts should be suitable, based either in Scripture or the content of already approved hymns. Many popular songs are appropriate, but a careful review of lyrics is mandatory, lest some unfortunate double entendre rear its head mid-verse.

Hymns and psalmody are appropriate, but unless the couple and the bulk of their friends and family are members of the congregation, experience shows it is best to keep these to a minimum, unless there is a competent choir capable of leading them or performing them as anthems. Instrumental or organ music is of course suitable to fill some of the transitions as the wedding party moves from one part of the church to another.

Receptions and Where They Happen

Some churches are able to host wedding receptions in their own facilities, in the parish hall or a garden space. Many couples will choose instead to hire a hall at another location, often one specializing in such events, with food and music provided. It is entirely at the discretion of clergy whether they choose to attend a wedding reception when invited; some couples may expect it and want the clergy to do an invocation or grace prior to a dinner. It is good to make sure this detail is worked out in advance in order to avoid disappointment or confusion.

Family and Friends

A center aisle can divide seating in the church with the family and friends of one of the couple on one side, those of the other on the opposite. How many friends and how distant the relations to invite are up to the couple to decide. The bare minimum is the two witnesses required by the church (and in many places, the state), though they usually function directly in the wedding as attendants to the couple. Parents often have a particular role, presenting one or both of the couple, and siblings (and sometimes children the couple already have) may figure as attendants or in some other capacity, such as reading one of the Scripture selections or singing a solo. This should all be thought through and set in advance, to minimize confusion on the day of the wedding.

The makeup of the assembly will play a role in determining whether to include the Eucharist as part of the celebration.

Sextons

Setting up for and cleaning up after a wedding can be a considerable chore, and a Saturday wedding may well leave the church in disarray for Sunday. It is not unusual for parishes to ask that there be a slight additional fee for the sexton, again depending on the custom of the place and the extent and size of the event.

Rings and Symbols

The wedding ring is one of the central symbols in marriage, and the exchange of rings is a powerful testimony to the mutual love, and the commitment to all of the responsibilities, that marriage entails. In recent years some other symbols have found their way into common use; some of them come from other cultures and may be appropriate as a way to honor a family tradition. Others, such as the "wedding candle" (in which the flames of two candles are simultaneously joined to light a third), seem to be novelties without the eloquence of the wedding ring—"without an end," as the old song about what a true love gives puts it. After all, the wedding candle is soon snuffed out, and leaves a very mixed message behind with the smoke. If a couple insist on having a wedding candle or some other supplemental symbol or symbolic act to celebrate their marriage, in addition to the ring(s) given or exchanged at the time of the vows, such a symbol might best be used at the wedding reception rather than in the wedding itself.

It is important to take the time to clarify who will be responsible for any ring or rings that are to be exchanged. Often the best man or some other senior attendant is responsible for the ring or rings, delivering them to the clergy in the course of the celebration. With weddings in which there is a ceremonial ring bearer (usually a child who carries the ring or rings on a pillow), it is common for the rings on the pillow to be inexpensive duplicates tied with a bow—the real rings safely kept in the best man's vest pocket.

Bulletins and Programs

Given the nature of these liturgies, and the likely participation in the congregation of people who may not be regular worshipers, or even churchgoers, it is advisable to produce a bulletin or program that is as complete as possible. Church Publishing Incorporated publishes the liturgies in booklet form, or the church may wish to customize and produce their own booklet. The goal is to be as helpful to the assembly as possible. A nicely designed program can be a lovely souvenir of the day, in addition to being a help through the celebration itself.

The Wedding Rehearsal

Need for a rehearsal is proportional to the complexity of the planned celebration. A simple liturgy involving only the officiant, the couple, and the witnesses may require no rehearsal at all, since the officiant can give direction on the spot. But the addition of music, supplemental attendants, flower girls or boys, ring bearers, and an expected congregation of family, friends, and well-wishers may complicate things and make including a rehearsal wise.

However, experience shows that the emotions of the day often lead participants to forget what they rehearsed, and they normally require some continued prompting by the officiant or another ceremonial guide.

It is also wise not to plan the rehearsal for the day just prior to the wedding. Having at least one day between the rehearsal and the wedding is a good provision for dealing with the many last-minute issues that almost always seem to arise to complicate even the best-planned wedding. The rehearsal should be planned to have as many of the participants as possible present. The scattered reality of some families may make this difficult, but it is good to have present at least the principal actors (the couple and their immediate attendants/witnesses), who can then be asked to fill any missing attendants in on the day—along with occasional nods and gentle verbal instruction from the clergy or another ceremonial guide.

The rehearsal may also be a convenient time to address any outstanding issues, and to make final preparations for the day itself.

Final Preparation

The wedding rehearsal is a good time for the couple to deliver their marriage license to the clergy, if that has not already taken place at one of the latter premarital sessions. If the clergy are required to return the executed license to the secular authorities, it will often come with a preaddressed envelope, and it is helpful if the couple include that along with the license itself. Licenses normally have to be returned to the issuing authority. Having the license in hand in this way (in advance) avoids the problem of someone leaving it at home on the day of the wedding.

About Arriving on Time

There is an old tradition that brides are entitled to keep grooms waiting at the chancel steps. However venerable the tradition, it is best avoided. Clergy should impress upon the couple the importance of a timely arrival for the celebration. It is discourteous to the wedding guests, and disrespectful to the clergy and musicians, the latter of whom may have other engagements or work that day.

Some clergy have found it helpful to ask couples to leave a token deposit, which will be refunded to them if the celebration begins on time, or partially contributed to the church in fifteen-minute increments. This may sound mercenary to some, but it does have a practical effect in reminding the couple that although this is an important day for them, others who are involved also have work and concerns to address. The amount forfeited can also accrue to organists or musicians in compensation for the additional draw on their time.

Walking Through the Liturgies

Before the Celebration

If all has gone according to plan—and that is not always the case—all decorations and preparations for the celebration will have been put in place the day before, or at the very latest well before the arrival of any wedding guests.

Wedding guests usually begin to arrive between half an hour and fifteen minutes prior to the celebration. It is very helpful if principal and other attendants can be on hand at least forty-five minutes prior to the event. Such attendants can serve as ushers to direct and seat the wedding guests. Some couples prefer to have their friends and family mingle, while others prefer to have them sit on different sides of the church (the left side of the nave facing the altar, to the liturgical "north," is by tradition the bride's side). Such details should be worked out in advance and the attendants instructed on how to seat the guests; if no attendants are available, the congregation may be able to provide volunteers to assist, or the couple could call upon guests they know will be in attendance to take on this role.

If one or both of the couple are to be sequestered (for example, the groom with the clergy, while the bride is with her bridesmaids or other attendants), it is helpful to work out a way for these separate groupings to communicate with each other. One of the members of the wedding party, a trusted friend, or a member of the congregation could be given this task. In situations where, for example, a groom is to enter the church with the clergy and stand at the head of the aisle prior to the arrival of any other members of the wedding party, it is helpful for them to know when to be in place, so as not to be left standing for an inordinate amount of time.

The following sections will walk through each of the two main types of liturgy, highlighting specific points and possibilities of each.

A Note on the Post-Celebration

Numerous customs have arisen about the various stages of the post-liturgical celebration(s). It is beyond the scope of this booklet to go into the many customs (from bouquet-tossing to cake-cutting), and this is best left to the family and the wedding planner to decide.

However, some things do normally take place right after the celebration, and it is good to highlight them here.

The custom of tossing rice at the couple derives from an ancient urge toward encouraging fertility. An urban legend holds that loose rice can injure birds who consume it, but it is actually more dangerous to people if they slip or fall due to excess rice on the pavement. The solution of putting rice in little cloth bags can lead to uncomfortable pelting of the couple. Some couples have substituted birdseed (also slippery), bubbles, flower petals, or sparklers (waved, not thrown) to add to the festivity. If anything is thrown at the couple, having someone available to tidy the grounds afterward is a wise precaution.

Post-liturgy photography is also possible, including posed pictures in the church, with the officiant. Most clergy make time to allow for this, and prefer it to photography during the celebration.

If the register and license have not been signed during the celebration, it is important that this be accomplished before the couple and their witnesses have left the premises.

The Celebration and Blessing of a Marriage (BCP and 2)

THE ENTRANCE

The ceremonial entry of the participants may seem to take longer than the rest of the ceremony; this is especially true if there is a large wedding party with many attendants. The entry can include multiple pieces of music to accompany the different groups and individuals, or be as simple as the couple chooses.

There are a number of ways to approach this entrance ceremony. One tradition is for the groom to enter unobtrusively with the best man and clergy (having been alerted by an appointed messenger to the fact that all is ready), and stand at the chancel or altar steps to await the arrival of the remainder of the wedding party, with the bride coming last of all, accompanied by her presenter/s (a father, another relative or friend, both parents) or alone. If this is the chosen form, the order of entry (not including the groom, best man, and clergy) could be:

❖ Bridesmaids escorted by ushers (groomsmen)

❖ Ring bearer (who may walk with or in front of the flower bearer)

❖ Flower bearer

❖ Maid (or matron) of honor

❖ Bride with father (or other escort) on her left

One charming custom, if the situation applies, is for the father of the bride to lift her veil and give her a kiss. This, like the "giving" of the bride, is a relic of the days in which a woman was under her father's custody until delivered to her husband. Some may prefer to omit such ceremonial references to the patriarchal system, while others may appreciate the symbolism reflecting parental (or paternal) affection.

This is by no means the only way for the wedding party to assemble. It is equally possible to have all but the couple enter first, and for the couple to enter from opposite sides and arrive at the designated place for the opening exhortation simultaneously. It is also possible to design the procession along the lines of the usual parish custom, with the couple and the cleric entering at the end.

The attendants of the couple should take up positions on either side, with room left for the couple themselves (the "bride's side" is to the clergy's right, and the congregation's left, on the "north side" in the old terminology). Since one of the aspects of the wedding is the joining of the couple, it is good to have some visible distance between them in the early part of the ceremony, with the space decreasing as they approach the point of making their vows.

A NOTE ON CHILDREN

If young children are taking part, with rings or flowers, one of the adult attendants should be assigned on each side to be their shepherd through the course of the ceremony.

OPENING EXHORTATION

The officiant then reads the opening text, facing the assembly (including the couple). This formal address lays out in concise language the church's teaching on God's purposes for, and the couple's responsibility in, marriage. It also serves, in the closing clauses, to determine that there is no impediment to the marriage known to either the community or the couple. It is customary for the officiant to pause briefly after the question to the assembly ("If any of you . . .") and the charge to the couple. Responses at this point are, fortunately, very rare. This portion of the rite is a vestige of the custom of the publication of banns. Some parishes continue that old custom (see the BCP, page 437) and the function is the same.

THE DECLARATION OF CONSENT

The celebrant then addresses each of the couple separately, confirming their intention and consent to marry, as well as once again highlighting the principal responsibilities of marriage. Each of the couple answers, "I will." The celebrant then asks the assembly to express their willingness to support the couple in their married life, and a rousing "We will" is expected.

PRESENTATION OR GIVING IN MARRIAGE

The presentation or "giving" of the bride (or groom, or both of the couple) is optional. If it is to take place, it does so in response to a simple question from the celebrant. Ceremonial at this point is minimal. (If a bride's father has not already lifted his daughter's veil to give a kiss, this might happen at this point; a mother might do similarly for a groom; or any combination of parents or older relatives for any other couple.) There should be no joining of hands at this point, however, and the couple themselves should remain at some distance from each other. The simplest and most effective physical action upon responding to the celebrant, "I (or we) do," is a slight bow and a step backward. The presenters may then take their seats.

The rubric provides for an interlude at this point, in the form of a hymn, psalm, or anthem. This is due in part to the fact that this generally marks a movement and transition, as the wedding party may at this time move into the choir area from the chancel steps. Instrumental music is also appropriate. Clergy can indicate it is time to move by stepping backward (with care) to allow the wedding party to move forward easily. If choir seating is available, the couple and their attendants continue to sit on opposite sides. A separate chair for each of the couple is sometimes added to highlight the uniqueness of the event.

Though there may be an urge to sit at this point, all should remain standing until the conclusion of the collect.

COLLECT

The celebrant may conveniently go to the altar for this, or simply continue to face the congregation. At the end of the collect all are seated for the reading(s) from Scripture.

SCRIPTURE READING(S)

At least one reading from Scripture is included here. The BCP rite lists the approved selections; CBM2, in addition to providing a somewhat different list, notes that other appropriate passages may be used. If communion is to be part of the celebration, the last (or only) reading will be from the Gospels.

If there is more than one reading, a psalm, hymn, or anthem may be sung or said. Unless the assembly is familiar with the hymnal, a psalm printed in the bulletin (to be read by the assembly, or by a reader, or responsively between them) or an anthem (which could be sung by a choir or soloist) is likely preferable.

Readers may be chosen from the friends of the family or from the wedding party. A deacon or other minister, if included, reads the Gospel. In the case of a mixed marriage, clergy from the tradition of one of the couple who wish to participate in the celebration might be invited to read the Gospel.

The Apostles' Creed may follow the reading(s) or the homily. It should be omitted if one of the couple is not baptized.

HOMILY

The homily is optional, but may provide the officiant with an opportunity to give a brief instruction on the nature of marriage, expand on the language of the exhortation, or highlight some aspect of the Scripture readings. In such a case the homily is best kept short, and it may be omitted. If the couple (and a majority of the assembly) are active members of the congregation, a longer homily is appropriate, but still shorter than a regular sermon.

THE EXCHANGE OF VOWS

Prior to the exchange of vows the officiant, couple, and their primary attendants move to the place at which the vows will be exchanged. This takes place most often at the altar rail, but other locations are possible, such as the chancel steps. The use of a "wedding prie-dieu" (a double-wide kneeler with an arm/book-rest) in a convenient and perhaps more visible location is also appropriate, considering the circumstances of the church's architecture.

At this point the couple will stand facing each other, and each will take the right hand of the other and recite the appointed text. This recitation can be committed to memory, but the officiant best prompts it, phrase by phrase. (The officiant may wish to mark a copy of the text with appropriate breaks for use in this circumstance.) It is important for each of the couple to actively *take* the hand of the other, and the other should not *offer* the hand but allow it to be *taken*. This also means loosing hands after the first recitation of vows. It is at this moment that the couple "take" each other in marriage, and the visual symbol is also an efficacious symbol. As the pronouncement of marriage will make clear, the joining of hands is the visible part of the public certification that the marriage is taking place, just as the vows offer verbal assurance.

The couple again loose their hands after the second of them has recited the vow.

BLESSING OF RING(S)

If rings are to be exchanged (CBM2 appears to require this, and the exchange of rings is one of the most enduring symbols of marriage; no other symbol seems to have the potency of the wedding ring), they may be blessed at this point. The rubric limits this blessing to the "Priest," so a deacon would omit this blessing if officiating.

The priest may hold out the copy of the prayer book being used, and the principal attendant (often the best man) will place the ring(s) on the open book. (In earlier days, this was also the point at which the "stole fee" was transmitted to the cleric.) The officiant may pronounce the blessing on the ring(s) from that position facing the couple, or take the ring(s) to the altar if it is nearby. (Blessed water and incense may be used if these are part of the tradition of the congregation or the couple.)

EXCHANGE OF RING(S)

On returning, the officiant can indicate with an extended finger which ring (still on the open book) is to be exchanged first. The giver places the ring on the ring finger of the other's hand while reciting the appointed text, again prompted by the officiant if that is desired. At this point the liturgies provide either the Trinitarian formula or a singular form; the latter is appropriate in the case of interfaith marriages.

JOINING OF HANDS AND PRONOUNCEMENT OF MARRIAGE

The officiant joins the (right) hands of the couple. At this point, the officiant may wish to wrap their stole around the couple's joined hands—this is the origin of the phrase "Tying the knot" when applied to marriage. (This means, among other things, that the officiant's stole is reachable, which would be the case if vested in cassock and surplice; and is of sufficient length.)

Because the officiant's hands are full at this moment, the recitation of the *fact* of marriage—the "pronouncement"—could be awkward if the officiant has not committed it to memory. (It is short enough that a card might be conveniently placed where the officiant can see it, if unwilling to commit it, or trust it, to memory.)

After the "Amen," most in the congregation will likely be expecting "You may kiss the bride," or a similar statement. However, in the 1979 revision of the marriage rite, that moment is deferred until after the prayers and blessing, in order to coincide with the peace.

THE SIGNING OF THE REGISTER

As noted earlier, the signing of the register is a requirement of church law (and the signing of the license may be required by civil law). Deferring this signing until after the ceremony can be perilous, as the couple and their witnesses may wish to rush off to the reception. This point in the ceremony seems to be a logical place, as the marriage has literally just happened. Placing the signing at this point also covers the hiccup of omitting the couple's first married kiss.

The register can be placed on a lectern so that the signers face the congregation as they sign. The license can also be placed on the facing page of the register for easy access, and marked with removable adhesive "flags" in different colors for the spouses and witnesses.

If the register and license are *not* signed at this point, it is vital that the officiant and couple have set the time and place for signing, and stick with that plan.

PRAYERS FOR THE COUPLE

The couple may remain at (or return to) the altar rail at this point, and prayers may be offered at the altar or another convenient place. The rubrics highlight the role of the deacon (or another person appointed) as the leader of the prayers that follow, though the officiant may be the best suited to this task in the absence of a deacon.

The prayers begin with the Lord's Prayer, unless communion follows. If there is no communion, one or more of the prayers may be omitted, and the prayer for the gift and heritage of children may be omitted in any case where such an omission is appropriate. (In the 1549 Book of Common Prayer, the equivalent prayer was to be omitted when the bride was past the age of childbearing.)

BLESSING OF THE MARRIAGE

The couple kneel once again (all others remain standing) and the officiant pronounces one of the two forms of blessing. The first draws on imagery from the Eastern Orthodox marriage liturgy (in which the couple are crowned and vested with a mantle around their shoulders) and has a distinctly Christian tone (including

allusion to the heavenly banquet). The second form focuses more upon the married life of the couple. The choice as to which form to use should be settled as part of the planning meeting.

In addition to one of these forms, the officiant (in the rubric named as "Priest" as a reminder that a deacon will omit this part of the liturgy if officiating) pronounces an explicitly Trinitarian blessing on the couple.

If it is the custom of the parish, blessed water and incense may also be used at this point.

THE PEACE

The celebrant's bidding the peace is optional, but this is the point in the liturgy when the couple exchange their first mutual greeting— usually a kiss—and greetings may be exchanged throughout the assembly.

If there is no communion to follow, the couple may then depart with festive music and some ceremony. No blessing or dismissal is included in the liturgy, although in some traditions a blessing of the couple's respective families is considered a part of the celebration. At the same time, this is not a moment at which to put the clergy forward, so the focus may be maintained on the couple as they depart, followed by their attendants.

IF COMMUNION FOLLOWS

The parish customary for the Eucharist is likely best maintained, with the following adjustments:

At the offertory, the couple may present the bread and wine and then remain at or near the altar rail to receive communion prior to other members of the assembly. It is helpful if the bread and wine are convenient to where the couple have been seated prior to the exchange of vows; a small table in the choir area is appropriate, and the couple can bring the elements to the deacon or celebrant with ease.

Unless the parish has a different custom, an offering from the congregation is not normally received. However, the couple may wish to make a contribution to the parish and dedicate an offering to the church at this point. If this is the case, ushers will need to be prepared in advance.

The BCP rite provides a proper preface in both Rite I and Rite II. CBM2 specifies that the preface is to be that of the season.

The liturgies provide a proper postcommunion prayer.

The departure of the couple is again a time for ceremonial and celebratory music.

There is a note in the previous section on other details of the departure, and events that take place after the wedding itself.

The Witnessing and Blessing of a Marriage

This liturgy differs in structure from the marriage liturgy of the Book of Common Prayer, and from the Celebration and Blessing of a Marriage 2, primarily in that it reflects the structure of other pastoral liturgies such as Baptism and Ordination. It is also structured so as to fit well with a celebration of the Holy Eucharist, including on a Sunday.

That being said, the individual elements or sections of the liturgy will generally have the same ceremonial options as in the BCP rite and its adaptation, although in some cases the sections themselves are in a different sequence.

It is important to note that this liturgy grows out of the process of developing a rite for blessing the lifelong covenant of a same-sex couple (prior to marriage equality being the law either of the state or the church). As part of that process, a number of mixed-sex couples expressed interest in using the rite, and in its current form (under trial use in accordance with the Constitution and Canons of the Episcopal Church) it is suitable to any couple.

Given the history of the development of this rite, it is also adaptable for use with couples who have made a prior lifelong commitment to each other.

THE ENTRANCE

The ceremonial entry of the participants can seem to take longer than the rest of the ceremony; this is especially true if there is a large wedding party with many attendants. The entry can include multiple pieces of music to accompany the different groups and individuals, or be as simple as the couple choose.

There are a number of ways to approach this entrance ceremony. One tradition is for one of the couple to enter unobtrusively with an attendant and the clergy (having been alerted by an appointed messenger to the fact that all is ready), and to stand at the chancel or altar steps to await the arrival of the remainder of the wedding party, with the intended spouse coming last of all, accompanied by a presenter or alone. If this is the chosen form, the order of entry (assuming one of the couple, attendant, and clergy are already in place) could be:

❖ Attendants, alone or in pairs

❖ Ring bearer (who may walk with or in front of a flower bearer)

❖ Flower bearer

❖ Attendant of honor

❖ Spouse with escort to the left

One charming custom, if the situation applies, is for the presenter to give a kiss to the one being presented. This is a relic of the days in which a woman was under her father's custody until delivered to her husband, and so will not be appropriate in all circumstances, but that is for the couple to decide. Some may prefer to omit such ceremonial references to the patriarchal system, while others may appreciate the symbolism reflecting parental (or paternal) affection.

This is by no means the only way for the wedding party to assemble. It is equally possible to have all but the couple enter first, and for the couple to enter from opposite sides and arrive at the designated place for the opening at the same time.

It is also possible to design the procession along the lines of the usual parish custom, with the couple and the cleric entering at the end. Given the eucharistic shape of this liturgy, that may be the best solution, and is particularly appropriate if the celebration takes place as part of the usual Sunday worship.

The attendants of the couple should take up positions on either side, with room left for the couple themselves (the "bride's side" is to the clergy's right, and the congregation's left, on the "north side" in the old terminology; for a same-sex couple such decisions are best left up to them). Since one of the aspects of the wedding is the joining of the couple, it is good to have some visible distance between them in the early part of the ceremony, with the space decreasing as they approach the point of making their vows.

A NOTE ON CHILDREN

If young children are taking part, with rings or flowers, one of the adult attendants should be assigned on each side to be their shepherd through the course of the ceremony.

OPENING GREETING AND EXHORTATION

The officiant then begins the rite with the customary eucharistic greeting.

There follow two optional exhortations, the second of which is suitable for couples who have made a prior lifelong covenant. As such an exhortation is so much an expected part of weddings, it is advised that the officiant make use of whichever is appropriate, facing the assembly (including the couple). These formal addresses lay out in concise language the church's teaching on the couple's responsibilities in marriage. They also serve, in the closing clauses, to invite prayer for the couple in living out their vows, and for the assembly to support them in their life together.

COLLECT OF THE DAY

This invitation naturally leads to the collect of the day. Several options for the collect itself are provided, including one in which children are included as part of the celebration. The celebrant may conveniently go to the altar for this, or simply continue to face the congregation. If the celebrant moves at this point, this may be the best time for the couple and their attendants also to move into the places where they will be seated. Clergy can indicate it is time to move by stepping backward (with care) to allow the wedding party to move forward easily. If choir seating is available, the couple and their attendants continue to sit on opposite sides. A separate chair for each of the couple is sometimes added to highlight the uniqueness of the event.

Alternatively, if the collect follows immediately with the celebrant still facing the assembly, all can move into the area in which they are to be seated for the reading(s) from Scripture after the Amen.

SCRIPTURE READING(S)

If they have not already done so, the couple and their attendants may move into the space reserved for their seating at this point, and each of the couple with their attendants continues to sit on opposite sides if that has been the pattern thus far.

At least one reading from Scripture is included here. The rite lists the approved selections; it notes that if the celebration is in the context of the Sunday Eucharist, the proper readings are used, except with the permission of the bishop. If communion is to be part of the celebration, a reading from the Gospels is included. The usual introductions for all of the readings are used, including the eucharistic form for the Gospel reading.

If there is more than one reading, a psalm, hymn, or anthem may be sung or said. Unless the assembly is familiar with the hymnal, a psalm printed in the bulletin (to be read by the assembly, or by a reader, or responsively between them) or an anthem (which could be sung by a choir or soloist) is likely preferable.

Readers may be chosen from the friends of the family or from the wedding party. A deacon or other minister, if included, reads the Gospel. In the case of a mixed marriage, clergy from the tradition of one of the couple who wish to participate in the celebration might be invited to read the Gospel.

The Apostles' Creed may follow the reading(s) or the sermon. It should be omitted if one of the couple is not baptized. (If a Sunday Eucharist, the Nicene Creed would be a normal part of the celebration.)

SERMON

A short sermon may provide the officiant with an opportunity to give a brief instruction on the nature of marriage, expanding on the language of the exhortation, or to highlight some aspect of the Scripture readings. If this is a normal Sunday Eucharist and the proper of the day is used, the sermon would naturally relate to the readings. In addition, if the couple (and a majority of the assembly) are active members of the congregation, a longer sermon is appropriate, but still best kept somewhat shorter than usual.

PRESENTATION

The presentation or "giving" of one or both of the couple is optional. If it is to take place, it does so in response to a simple question from the celebrant. Ceremonial at this point is minimal. (If a presenter has not already given an embrace to the one being presented, this might happen now; this is true of any combination of parents or older relatives, friends, or members of the assembly.) There should be no joining of hands at this point, however, and the couple themselves should remain at some distance from each other.

The officiant asks an additional question of the presenters, similar to that asked of sponsors at baptism, and they respond with an affirmation of support.

No further ceremony is needed at this point, and the presenters may return to their seats. Some have suggested the presenters should remain with the couple through what follows, but this tends to muddy the clarity that separates the presentation from the couple's action in speaking for themselves—as indeed they must at this point, since this is the essence of consent and commitment.

DECLARATION OF CONSENT

Because of the action that follows, this is likely a good time for the couple to approach the place at which they will exchange their vows, usually the altar rail or a wedding prie-dieu set in a convenient place. They should face the officiant at this point, still at some slight distance from each other.

The officiant then addresses the couple jointly with a brief affirmation of the reason for their presence: to exchange vows and bid the church's blessing. In this and the following dialogue, there is optional language for those who are renewing or continuing in their committed relationship.

The presider then addresses each of the couple individually, determining their free and unconditional consent in offering each to the other, with the promise of lifelong fidelity. This question and response sound the three principal notes alluded to in the declaration the couple signed prior to the wedding, in which they expressed their understanding that their marriage is to be "unconditional, mutual, exclusive, faithful, and lifelong." Each of the couple affirms their willingness, with God's help, to realize these promises.

At this point the whole assembly stands, and the couple turn to face them. The officiant addresses the assembly to ask them if they will do all in their power to uphold and honor the couple in their commitment, and the assembly should answer with a firm, clear, and unqualified, "We will." The officiant then asks the assembly to affirm its commitment to prayer, in times of trouble as well as of joy. With their response in the affirmative, the officiant then calls them to prayer for the couple and the community.

PRAYERS FOR THE COUPLE AND COMMUNITY

A deacon or another leader leads the prayers, though the officiant may be the best suited to this task in the absence of a deacon or another leader trained in leading public prayer.

The form of the prayers is flexible, but the form provided is a good outline. The intercessions begin with a set of eight petitions for the couple; among those petitions, the prayer for children entrusted to them by God may be omitted. (In the 1549 Book of Common Prayer the equivalent prayer was to be omitted when the bride was past the age of childbearing.) If the liturgy takes place as part of the Sunday Eucharist, the usual form of the Prayers of the People may follow the initial intercessions concerning the couple. On other occasions the shorter version of prayers for the community and the world may be used, or may be omitted or abridged. The couple and clergy should take care to work out this form of prayer in advance.

The officiant concludes the prayers with the collect provided or another appropriate collect. If there is not to be a communion, the Lord's Prayer is then introduced and recited by the assembly; it is omitted if communion follows.

THE EXCHANGE OF VOWS

The assembly may be seated at this point. Prior to the exchange of vows the officiant, couple, and their primary attendants move to the place at which the vows will be exchanged, if they have not already done so at the beginning of the prayers. This exchange of vows takes place most often at the altar rail, but other locations are possible, such as the chancel steps. The use of a "wedding prie-dieu" (a double-wide kneeler with an arm/book-rest) in a convenient and perhaps more visible location is also appropriate, considering the circumstances of the church's architecture.

At this point the couple will stand facing each other, and the officiant will deliver a short invitation to them to make their covenant in the light of God's word and the comforting prayer of the community.

Each of the couple in turn will take the right hand of the other and recite one of the two forms of the appointed text. (The second form is most appropriate in the case where one of the couple is not baptized.) The officiant, phrase by phrase, best prompts this recitation. (The officiant may wish to mark a copy of the text with appropriate breaks for use in this circumstance.)

It is important for each of the couple actively to *take* the hand of the other, and the other should not *offer* the hand but allow it to be *taken*. This also means loosing hands after the first recitation of vows. It is at this moment that the couple "take" each other in marriage, and the visual symbol is also an efficacious one.

The couple again loose their hands after the second of them has recited the vow.

BLESSING OF RING(S)

If rings (or some other symbol) are to be exchanged, they are presented to the officiant at this point. The exchange of rings is one of the most enduring symbols of marriage; no other symbol seems to have the potency of the wedding ring.

The officiant may hold out the copy of the prayer book being used, and one of the principal attendants who has had the ring(s) in charge will place the ring(s) on the open book. (In earlier days, this was also the point at which the "stole fee" was transmitted to the cleric.) The officiant may pronounce the blessing from that position facing the couple, or take the ring(s) to the altar if it is nearby. (Blessed water and incense may be used if these are part of the tradition of the congregation or the couple.)

EXCHANGE OF RING(S)

After bidding this blessing, the officiant can indicate with an extended finger which ring (still on the open book) is to be exchanged first. The giver places the ring on the ring finger of the other's hand while reciting the appointed text, again prompted by the officiant if that is desired. At this point the rite provides either a singular or Trinitarian conclusion; the former is more appropriate in the case of interfaith marriages.

If the couple had exchanged and worn rings previously, as a sign of their commitment, the presider may bless the rings on the couple's hands, using the form provided.

JOINING OF HANDS AND PRONOUNCEMENT OF MARRIAGE

The officiant joins the (right) hands of the couple. At this point, the officiant may wish to wrap the stole around the couple's joined hands—this is the origin of the phrase "Tying the knot" when applied to marriage. (This means, among other things, that the officiant's stole is reachable, which would be the case if vested in cassock and surplice. It also would have to be of sufficient length and narrowness to slide out easily and wrap around the pair of hands.)

Because the officiant's hands are full at this moment, whether the stole is used or not, the recitation of the *fact* of marriage—the "pronouncement"—could be awkward if the officiant has not committed it to memory. (It is short enough that a card might be conveniently placed where the officiant can see it, if unwilling to commit it, or trust it, to memory.) The reference to the civil jurisdiction is optional.

THE SIGNING OF THE REGISTER

As noted earlier, the signing of the register is a requirement of church law (and the signing of the license may be required by civil law). Deferring this signing until after the ceremony can be perilous, as the couple and their witnesses may wish to rush off to the reception. This point in the ceremony seems to be a logical place, as the marriage has literally just happened. It could also take place after the peace and prior to the offertory (if communion is to follow) or the final blessing and dismissal (if communion is not to follow).

The register can be placed on a lectern so that the signers face the congregation as they sign. The license can also be placed on the facing page of the register for easy access and marked with removable adhesive "flags" in different colors for the spouses and witnesses.

If the register and license are *not* signed at this point, or immediately after the peace, it is vital that the officiant and couple have set the time and place for signing, and stick with that plan.

BLESSING OF THE COUPLE

The couple kneel or remain standing, and the officiant offers a short prayer followed by one of the two forms of blessing. The first names the Persons of the Trinity, but is otherwise identical to the second. Blessed water and incense may be used if that is a custom of the couple or the parish.

THE PEACE AND WHAT FOLLOWS

The presider bids the peace at this point, using one of the forms provided. This is the moment in the liturgy when the couple exchange their first mutual greeting—usually a kiss—and greetings may be exchanged throughout the assembly.

As noted previously, if the parish register has not been signed earlier, this moment provides another convenient time to do so.

If there is no communion to follow, the presider blesses and the deacon (or presider) dismisses the assembly; the couple and their attendants may then depart with festive music and some ceremony. In some traditions a blessing of the couple's respective families is considered a part of the celebration, and it might well take place prior to the final blessing.

IF THE EUCHARIST FOLLOWS

After the peace (and signing of the register, if done at this point), the liturgy continues with the offertory. The parish customary for the Eucharist is likely best maintained, with the following adjustments:

At the offertory, the couple may present the bread and wine, which can be ready beforehand on a small table conveniently placed. They then remain at or near the altar rail to receive communion prior to other members of the assembly.

Unless the parish has a different custom, an offering from the congregation is not normally received. (Obviously, if this is the Sunday Eucharist the ordinary collection will be received.) However, even when it is not a Sunday celebration, the couple may wish to make a contribution to the parish and dedicate an offering to the church at this point. If this is the case, ushers will need to be prepared in advance.

A proper preface is provided, as is a proper postcommunion prayer. Both are optional, and a seasonal preface and the customary postcommunion prayer may be used instead.

The departure of the couple is again a time for ceremonial and celebratory music.

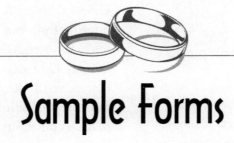

Sample Forms

Marriage Information and Application

_____ Episcopal Church

_____ (Address)

_____ (City) _____ (State) _____ (Zip)

_____ (Phone) _____ (E-mail)

Marriage is a solemn rite of the church, a deeply personal matter affecting two people (and their families), and—in this jurisdiction—a matter of civil law. This document will give you some important information about marriage, and the attached forms will gather the information needed from you. An additional form will assist in planning the ceremony. **Please don't fill out any of the forms except the _personal information sections for the spouses_ until you have met with the priest.** The forms are provided here for your information only.

THE CHURCH'S TEACHING AND REQUIREMENTS

Marriage is a solemn and public covenant made in the presence of God. The church holds marriage to be a lifelong union, in heart, body, and mind, intended by God for mutual joy; for the help and comfort given one another in prosperity and adversity; and, when it is God's will, for the gift and heritage of children, and their nurture in the knowledge and love of the Lord. You will both sign a declaration that you understand this teaching and intend to make your best effort to fulfill it, with God's help. The declaration is included as part of this application. (Please don't fill it out until after your premarriage instruction sessions with the priest.)

The church requires the following:

❖ At least one of you must be baptized. (There are additional requirements for interfaith marriage, and for marriages between an Episcopalian and a member of the Roman Catholic Church. If either of these apply, please bring this to the clergy's attention. Note that the Roman Catholic Church does not recognize marriages performed by Episcopal clergy for members of the Roman Catholic Church unless a dispensation has been obtained.)

❖ You must apply for marriage no less than thirty days before the ceremony is to take place. (This requirement may be waived if at least one of you is a member of the parish, or good reason exists to shorten the time.)

❖ Both of you must have the legal right to contract marriage (age, termination of previous marriages, etc.).

❖ You must obtain a license and deliver it to the priest no less than two weeks before the marriage.

❖ You must certify to the priest that you freely and knowingly consent to the marriage, without fraud, coercion, mistake as to identity, or mental reservation.

❖ You must receive instruction from the clergy (or someone known to them) on the nature, meaning, and purpose of marriage. This involves from three to five 45-minute sessions, arranged at an agreed time. The final session may also include time spent planning the liturgy. Both of you must be present for all sessions.

❖ At least two witnesses must be present at the solemnization.

It lies within the discretion of the clergy to decline to solemnize or bless any marriage.

When either spouse has been married to a person still living, the following requirements come into play:

❖ The clergy must examine the documentation and evidence that any prior marriage has been annulled or dissolved by a final judgment or decree of a civil court of competent jurisdiction. These papers may be presented at the time of application, or at the first session of marriage instruction.

❖ You are advised that continuing concern must be shown for the well-being of the former spouse and any children of the prior marriage.

❖ The permission of the bishop must be obtained *before* the marriage may be solemnized. This requires the completion of an application for remarriage, which must be submitted to the bishop **no less than eight weeks** prior to the wedding. This form is normally prepared at one of the premarriage sessions with the clergy, which must therefore take place **no less than nine weeks** prior to the intended marriage date.

By completing this application, you signify your understanding of the foregoing, and your willingness to abide by these conditions and fulfill these requirements.

_____
Signature

_____
Signature

Information Concerning the Couple

<table>
<tr><td></td><td>Date of Application</td><td></td></tr>
<tr><td rowspan="7">Spouse A's Personal Information</td><td>Full name</td><td></td></tr>
<tr><td>Address</td><td></td></tr>
<tr><td>Telephone / e-mail</td><td></td></tr>
<tr><td>Date and place of birth</td><td></td></tr>
<tr><td>Father's name</td><td></td></tr>
<tr><td>Mother's maiden name</td><td></td></tr>
<tr><td>Parents' residence</td><td></td></tr>
<tr><td rowspan="7">Spouse A's Marital Status</td><td colspan="2">☐ Never married   ☐ Widowed   ☐ Divorced   Number of this intended marriage:</td></tr>
<tr><td colspan="2">Date and place of previous marriage:</td></tr>
<tr><td colspan="2">Ages of children of previous marriage:</td></tr>
<tr><td colspan="2">Have you any obligations regarding the well-being of your former spouse or children? ☐ Yes ☐ No</td></tr>
<tr><td colspan="2">Are you carrying out these responsibilities? ☐ Yes ☐ No   Do you plan to continue? ☐ Yes ☐ No</td></tr>
<tr><td colspan="2">Date and place of divorce decree / annulment:</td></tr>
<tr><td colspan="2">Permission from bishop to remarry [clergy fill in info here]</td></tr>
<tr><td rowspan="4">Spouse A's Church Status</td><td colspan="2">☐ Baptized in the   Church</td></tr>
<tr><td colspan="2">☐ Confirmed in the   Church</td></tr>
<tr><td colspan="2">☐ Communicant of the   Church</td></tr>
<tr><td colspan="2">Name of parish / congregation:</td></tr>
</table>

INFORMATION CONCERNING THE COUPLE, continued

<table>
<tr><td rowspan="7">Spouse B's
Personal Information</td><td>Full name</td><td></td></tr>
<tr><td>Address</td><td></td></tr>
<tr><td>Telephone / e-mail</td><td></td></tr>
<tr><td>Date and place of birth</td><td></td></tr>
<tr><td>Father's name</td><td></td></tr>
<tr><td>Mother's maiden name</td><td></td></tr>
<tr><td>Parents' residence</td><td></td></tr>
<tr><td rowspan="7">Spouse B's
Marital Status</td><td colspan="2">☐ Never married   ☐ Widowed   ☐ Divorced   Number of this intended marriage:</td></tr>
<tr><td colspan="2">Date and place of previous marriage:</td></tr>
<tr><td colspan="2">Ages of children of previous marriage:</td></tr>
<tr><td colspan="2">Have you any obligations regarding the well-being of your former spouse or children?   ☐ Yes   ☐ No</td></tr>
<tr><td colspan="2">Are you carrying out these responsibilities?   ☐ Yes   ☐ No   Do you plan to continue?   ☐ Yes   ☐ No</td></tr>
<tr><td colspan="2">Date and place of divorce decree / annulment:</td></tr>
<tr><td colspan="2">Permission from bishop to remarry [clergy fill in info here]</td></tr>
<tr><td rowspan="4">Spouse B's
Church Status</td><td colspan="2">☐ Baptized in the   Church</td></tr>
<tr><td colspan="2">☐ Confirmed in the   Church</td></tr>
<tr><td colspan="2">☐ Communicant of the   Church</td></tr>
<tr><td colspan="2">Name of parish / congregation:</td></tr>
<tr><td colspan="3">Marriage license #:   Where issued:</td></tr>
<tr><td colspan="3">Address of couple after marriage:</td></tr>
</table>

Concerning the Ceremony

The Episcopal marriage rites are among the most beautiful services of the church. The clergy are responsible for ensuring the dignity of the service, and have final authority over all aspects of the conduct of the service. They will do their best, working with you in planning the celebration, to accommodate your wishes within the limits of church authority.

THE RITE

Except in interfaith marriages (for which another option is available), the service will be one of the following:

- ❖ The Celebration and Blessing of a Marriage
- ❖ The Celebration and Blessing of a Marriage 2
- ❖ The Witnessing and Blessing of a Marriage

In addition to choosing the rite that is appropriate, there are also many options within each of these rites. The wording of the vows, however, may not be altered. Celebration of the Holy Eucharist is optional. Note it is inappropriate to have communion "just for the bride and groom"—if there is a communion, all are invited to take part.

The priest is solely responsible for the conduct of the service, and pronounces the blessing (and celebrates the Eucharist). Other assisting ministers may take part, in consultation with the priest. The couple may choose a family member or friend to read one or two scriptural readings. The priest or a deacon reads the Gospel.

MUSIC

If you wish to have music for your wedding, **you must contact the parish organist,** who has right of first refusal for all weddings. The organist's fee and any other music costs (for soloists) must be paid by cash or money order **no later than the wedding rehearsal.** If the parish organist is unavailable, a substitute may be arranged with the organist's permission. All arrangements for singers or instrumentalists *must* be made through the parish organist. All vocal music must have the priest's approval. Popular songs may be allowed if the lyrics conform to Scripture.

PHOTOGRAPHY

The services of a professional photographer may be engaged, but no photography is permitted in the sanctuary.

REHEARSAL

A rehearsal is required within the week prior to the ceremony. All major participants (the couple, principal attendants, and parents if they are participating) must be present. Rehearsal normally takes no more than forty-five minutes. A copy of the wedding invitation must be sent to the priest.

TIMELINESS

The time for the wedding must be chosen with care. To encourage timeliness, a $200 cash deposit is required at the wedding rehearsal. This will be returned at the wedding itself, less $50 for each fifteen minutes of lateness up to one hour. If the wedding party is not ready to begin within one hour from the appointed time, **the wedding will be cancelled and you will forfeit the deposit and any fees.**

FEES

All fees (and lateness deposit) are due no later than the wedding rehearsal.

❖ **Clergy:** Clergy prepare couples and celebrate weddings as part of their ministry, and do not charge a fee.

❖ **Music:** The organist's fee of $200 is for a standard service, including music for up to one-half hour prior to the wedding. A more elaborate ceremony will be subject to an extra charge. The couple is responsible for the fees for any instrumentalists or singers whose services have been arranged in consultation with the parish organist. The organist may have other engagements, and it is imperative that services be arranged as soon as possible. The clergy can provide you the parish organist's contact information.

❖ **Flowers:** The couple are responsible for all expenses relating to flowers or other decorations, and arranging for the delivery of flowers to the church.

❖ **Sexton:** A standard charge of $100, payable to the parish, will cover the additional costs incurred for cleaning the church before and after the ceremony.

❖ **Church:** A donation of at least $500 to the parish (not including the sexton's fee) is required. If able to do so, it is recommended that couples consider a larger donation of 5–10 percent (the biblical tithe) of what will be spent on the wedding reception.

❖ **Late fee:** A cash deposit of $200 will be refunded after the wedding if it starts on time. For every fifteen minutes of lateness, $50 will be retained by the church to compensate the organist and staff for this inconvenience.

❖ **The total cost of $1,000** ($200 of which is the refundable cash late fee) is due no later than the wedding rehearsal. The couple may wish to pay these costs over the weeks leading up to the wedding.

Guide to Planning the Liturgy: Celebration and Blessing of a Marriage

Spouse A Full Name		
Spouse B Full Name		
Witnesses	1) Name and address:	
	2) Name and address:	
Wedding Location	(if not the church):	
Wedding Date:		Time:
Rehearsal Date:		Time:
The Service (* = required)	Prelude	
	Entrance Hymn	
	Music for the entrance	
	Opening Exhortation and The Declaration of Consent*	
	Presentation or giving in marriage	Name of presenter(s):
	Hymn, Psalm, or Anthem	
	Collect*	
	Scripture Readings (One or more readings may be used, with a psalm, hymn, or anthem between them.)	☐ Genesis 1:26–28 (Male and female he created them) ☐ Genesis 2:4–9, 15–24 (They become one flesh) ☐ Song of Solomon 2:10–13; 8:6–7 (Love is unquenchable) ☐ Tobit 8:5b–8 NEB (That she and I may grow old together)
	Reader(s): _____ _____	☐ 1 Corinthians 13:1–13 (Love is patient and kind) ☐ Ephesians 3:14–19 (. . . from whom every family is named) ☐ Ephesians 5:1–2, 21–33 (Walk in love, as Christ loved us) ☐ Colossians 3:12–17 (Love binds all together in harmony) ☐ 1 John 4:7–16 (Let us love one another for love is of God)
	Psalm	☐ Psalm 67 ☐ Psalm 127 ☐ Psalm 128
	Hymn or Anthem	
	Gospel (*Required if communion follows) Minister: _____	☐ Matthew 5:1–10 (The Beatitudes) ☐ Matthew 5:13–16 (Let your light so shine) ☐ Matthew 7:21, 24–29 (Like a wise man who built on rock) ☐ Mark 10:6–9, 13–16 (They are no longer two, but one) ☐ John 15:9–12 (Love one another as I have loved you)

	Homily (preceded or followed by the Apostles' Creed)	
	The Exchange of Vows*	
	Blessing of Ring(s)	
	Exchange of Ring(s)*	
	Joining of hands and pronouncement of marriage*	
	The Signing of the Register*	
	The Lord's Prayer	(may be omitted if communion is to follow)
	Prayers for the Couple* (one or more may be omitted, unless communion follows)	
	Blessing of the Marriage*	☐ Form 1 or ☐ Form 2, followed by the closing blessing
	The Peace	
	The couple's mutual greeting* (which may extend to the congregation)	
	Departure of the wedding party, unless communion follows	
	Music for departure	
Holy Communion	Offertory Hymn	
	Great Thanksgiving	
	Sanctus (may be said or sung)	
	Fraction Anthem	
	Music during communion	
	Postcommunion Hymn	
	Postcommunion Prayer	
	Music for departure	

Guide to Planning the Liturgy: Celebration and Blessing of a Marriage 2

Spouse A Full Name		
Spouse B Full Name		
Witnesses	1) Name and address:	
	2) Name and address:	
Wedding Location	(if not the church):	
Wedding Date:		Time:
Rehearsal Date:		Time:
The Service (* = required)	Prelude	
	Entrance Hymn	
	Music for the entrance	
	Opening Exhortation and The Declaration of Consent*	
	Presentation or giving in marriage	Name of presenter(s):
	Hymn, Psalm, or Anthem	
	Collect*	
	Scripture Readings (One or more readings may be used, with a psalm, hymn, or anthem between them.)	☐ Genesis 1:26–28 (Male and female he created them) ☐ Song of Solomon 2:10–13; 8:6–7 (Love is unquenchable) ☐ Tobit 8:5b–8 NEB (That she and I may grow old together)
	Reader(s): _____ _____	☐ 1 Corinthians 13:1–13 (Love is patient and kind) ☐ Ephesians 3:14–19 (. . . from whom every family is named) ☐ Ephesians 5:1–2 (Walk in love, as Christ loved us) ☐ Colossians 3:12–17 (Love binds all together in harmony) ☐ 1 John 4:7–16 (Let us love one another for love is of God)
	Psalm	☐ Psalm 67 ☐ Psalm 127 ☐ Psalm 128
	Hymn or Anthem	
	Gospel (*Required if communion follows) Minister: _____	☐ Matthew 5:1–10 (The Beatitudes) ☐ Matthew 5:13–16 (Let your light so shine) ☐ Matthew 7:21, 24–29 (Like a wise man who built on rock) ☐ John 15:9–12 (Love one another as I have loved you)

	Homily or other response to the Readings (preceded or followed by the Apostles' Creed)	
	The Exchange of Vows*	
	Blessing of Ring(s or other symbol)	
	Exchange of Ring(s or other symbol)*	
	Joining of hands and pronouncement of marriage*	
	The Signing of the Register*	
	The Lord's Prayer	(may be omitted if communion is to follow)
	Prayers for the Couple* (one or more may be omitted, unless communion follows)	
	Blessing of the Marriage*	☐ Form 1 or ☐ Form 2, followed by the closing blessing
	The Peace	
	The couple's mutual greeting* (which may extend to the congregation)	
	Departure of the wedding party, unless communion follows	
	Music for departure	
Holy Communion	Offertory Hymn	
	Great Thanksgiving	
	Sanctus (may be said or sung)	
	Fraction Anthem	
	Music during communion	
	Postcommunion Hymn	
	Postcommunion Prayer	
	Music for departure	

Guide to Planning the Liturgy:
Witnessing and Blessing of a Marriage

Spouse A Full Name		
Spouse B Full Name		
Witnesses	1) Name and address:	
	2) Name and address:	
Wedding Location	(if not the church):	
Wedding Date:		Time:
Rehearsal Date:		Time:
The Service (* = required)	Prelude	
	Entrance Hymn	
	Music for the entrance	
	Opening Greeting and Exhortation*	
	Collect of the Day*	☐ Form 1 ☐ Form 2 ☐ Form 3 ☐ Form 4
	Scripture Readings* (One or more readings, each followed by a psalm, hymn, or anthem) Note: If the celebration is part of the Sunday Eucharist, the Sunday readings are used, except with the permission of the bishop. Reader(s): _____ _____	☐ Ruth 1:16–17 ☐ 1 Samuel 18:1b, 3; 20:16–17, 42a ☐ 1 Samuel 18:1–4 ☐ Song of Solomon 2:10–13; 8:6–7 ☐ Micah 4:1–4
		☐ Romans 12:9–18 ☐ 1 Corinthians 12:31b–13:13 ☐ Galatians 5:14, 22–26 ☐ Ephesians 3:14–21 ☐ Colossians 3:12–17 ☐ 1 John 3:18–24 ☐ 1 John 4:7–16, 21
	Psalm	☐ Psalm 65 ☐ Psalm 67 ☐ Psalm 85:7–13 ☐ Psalm 98 ☐ Psalm 100 ☐ Psalm 126 ☐ Psalm 127 ☐ Psalm 133 ☐ Psalm 148 ☐ Psalm 149:1–5
	Hymn or Anthem	
	Gospel (*Required if communion follows) Minister: _____	☐ Matthew 5:1–16 ☐ Mark 12:28–34 ☐ Luke 6:32–38 ☐ John 15:9–17 ☐ John 17:1–2, 18–26

	Sermon*	
	Presentation or giving in marriage	Name of presenter(s):
	Declaration of Consent*	
	Prayers for the couple and community*	
	The Lord's Prayer	(omitted if communion is to follow)
	The Exchange of Vows*	
	Blessing of Ring(s)	
	Exchange of Ring(s) (Note: If couple have already exchanged rings, a form is provided.)	
	Joining of hands and pronouncement of marriage*	
	The Signing of the Register*	
	Blessing of the Couple*	Invocation followed by ☐ Form 1 or ☐ Form 2
	The Peace (and Blessing of the People and dismissal, unless communion follows)	
	Departure of the wedding party, unless communion follows	
	Music for departure	
Holy Communion	Offertory Hymn	
	Proper Preface and Great Thanksgiving	
	Sanctus (may be said or sung)	
	Fraction Anthem	
	Music during communion	
	Postcommunion Hymn	
	Postcommunion Prayer	
	Music for departure	

In the Name of the Father, and of the Son, and of the Holy Spirit. Amen.

☩

The Declaration of Intention

together with

the Certification of Capacity and Consent

In accordance with the Canons of the Episcopal Church

and

Agreement to abide by the Marriage Guidelines
of _____

We understand the teaching of the church that God's purpose for our marriage
is for our mutual joy, for the help and comfort we will give to each other in
prosperity and adversity, and, when it is God's will,
for the gift and heritage of children
and their nurture in the knowledge and love of God.
We also understand that our marriage is to be unconditional, mutual, exclusive,
faithful, and lifelong; and we engage to make the utmost effort
to accept these gifts and fulfill these duties,
with the help of God and the support of our community.

Certification of Capacity and Consent

We do hereby affirm that both of us have the right to contract a marriage
according to the laws of the *State* of _____;
and that we do both freely and knowingly consent to such marriage,
without fraud, coercion, mistake as to identity of a partner, or mental reservation.

Agreement to Abide by the Marriage Guidelines of _____
We the undersigned, desiring to be married on _____ at _____,
have read the accompanying guidelines "Concerning the Ceremony" and hereby
covenant to abide by them.

_____   _____
Signature of Spouse   *Signature of Spouse*

_____   _____
Date   *Attest*

A Traditional Wedding Service

ABOUT THIS ARTICLE

The language and terminology used in this article are self-consciously *traditional*. The intention is to provide a sort of historical snapshot of what a marriage might have looked like fifty years ago. Much has changed since then, and a contemporary couple, working with their clergy, can use this template as closely or as loosely as they wish, adapting the traditional language to suit their own circumstances. Very little in the marriage liturgy is set in stone (the vows themselves being of that sort)—but having a clear starting place is the best way to move forward in adaptation. This outline is presented in that spirit.

BEFORE THE SERVICE

Prior to the service, the groom joins the priest in the sacristy. The ushers (groomsmen) seat those arriving on the bride's and groom's sides of the church (left and right respectively), leaving a single seat vacant in the front row on each side for the father of the bride (or the person "giving the bride away") and the mother of the groom (if present). The last person to be seated is the mother of the groom, who is escorted by the best man. The best man then goes to the sacristy to join the groom and priest. This is the signal that all is ready to begin.

The best man, groom, and priest enter from the sacristy and go directly to their places. This is the signal that the procession may begin.

THE PROCESSION

The bridesmaids enter first, escorted by the ushers (groomsmen), and they take up their places to the left and right, filling in from the outside in. The ring bearer (who may walk with or in front of the flower bearer) takes his place next to the best man, who can keep an eye on him. The flower bearer will stand next to the innermost bridesmaid. The maid of honor takes up a place opposite the best man. When the bride enters, her father (or other escort) is on her left. She takes her place opposite the groom, staying still rather far apart from him. Her father stands directly behind her.

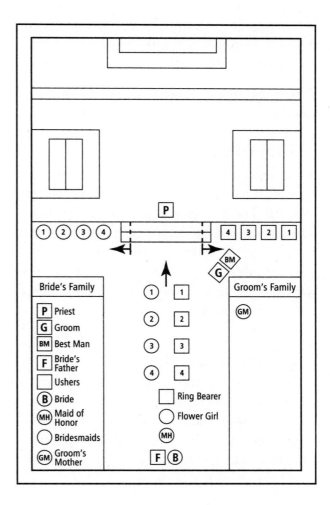

THE OPENING

All remain in place for the exhortation and examination. At the presentation or "giving" of the bride, the bride's father steps to the center (to his daughter's right), and answers "I do" while taking his daughter's right hand. He then steps back and is seated opposite the groom's mother on the left side of the church.

The priest will then take a step backward, indicating that the bridal party is to enter the chancel. The bride and groom step up first, taking the chairs set for them in front of the choir seats. The groomsmen and bride's party move up and into the choir seats, with the best man and maid of honor leading the way, and ending up in the seats nearest to the altar. All remain standing.

After the opening prayer all are seated for the reading from Scripture. All stand for the Gospel.

THE MARRIAGE

The priest invites the bride and groom, and the best man and maid of honor, to come to the altar rail. The bride and groom face each other. The man then takes the woman's right hand in his and says the marriage vows phrase by phrase after the priest. He then lets go of her hand. The woman then takes the man's right hand in hers, says the marriage vows, and looses his hand.

The best man then lays the ring(s) on the book, presented by the priest. The priest takes the ring(s) to the altar and blesses them, and then returns to the couple. He presents the woman's ring to the man, and he puts it on the woman's ring finger, saying the formula after the priest. The woman then does the same.

The priest then joins the hands of the couple, wraps them with the stole, and pronounces them to be married.

The couple and their attendants then go to the place designated to sign the register.

THE PRAYERS AND BLESSING

After all return to their place at the rail, a person appointed leads the prayers. The people remain standing, the couple kneel, and the priest blesses them. They then stand, and the priest delivers the peace, at which point the husband and wife kiss.

THE COMMUNION AND CONCLUSION

All is as at an ordinary communion, except that the bread and wine are presented to the priest by the husband and wife. In addition, the husband and wife receive communion first.

After communion all return to their places. All stand for the final blessing and dismissal.

For the retiring procession, the husband and wife go first, followed by the best man and maid of honor, and then the other attendants in pairs, in reverse order of entry (the first to have entered will be the last to leave). It is good for the ring bearer and flower bearer, and any other small children involved in the service, to be with one of the adult members of the party.

Glossary

annulment—A formal declaration, in either church or civil law, that a former marriage was invalid and hence not properly constituted.

banns—A public statement of a couple's intent to marry, usually *published* as part of Sunday worship.

baptism—The sacrament by which a person becomes a member of the body of Christ.

blessing—The act of invoking the name of God upon a person(s), place(s), or thing(s) in petition for their well-being; the form of words used in this invocation.

canon—A rule or law of the church.

cassock (and surplice)—A form of liturgical dress consisting of a full-length, long-sleeved robe (usually black) worn under a loosely fitting, long-sleeved white over-vestment.

catechumenate—The period of preparation for baptism.

celebrant—The officiant.

chancel—The area of the church near the altar.

civil—Under the governance of the city, state, or nation.

cleric—An ordained minister.

confirmation—The rite by which a person makes an adult commitment to the Christian faith.

consent, declaration of—A document certifying that a couple understand and consent to the requirements of the church concerning their marriage.

customary—A descriptive outline of the ceremonial used in a particular church.

deacon—An ordained minister who serves in the liturgy and mission of the church, with particular responsibilities different from those assigned to priests and bishops. In some jurisdictions a deacon may be authorized to officiate at a wedding.

dispensation—A relaxation of a rule permitting some action to go forward.

exhortation—An instructive address delivered by the officiant, briefly laying out an explanation of what is to take place.

General Convention—The governing body of the Episcopal Church.

Gospel—In a liturgical context, the Scripture reading taken from one of the four Gospels.

Holy Communion / Holy Eucharist—The sacrament by which Christians share in the body and blood of Christ.

jurisdiction—An area of responsibility and authority.

liturgy—The ceremony and ritual activity of the church.

officiant—The person responsible for the conduct of the liturgy.

ordination—The rite by which a person is set apart for a particular ministry in the church.

nave—The main body of the church in which the congregation is seated.

New Testament—The writings of the early followers of Christ, codified as part of the Christian Bible.

Old Testament—The Hebrew Scriptures.

pastoral rites—Liturgies reflecting a primarily personal focus, including marriage, ministry with the sick, and burial.

peace, the—The moment in the liturgy when members of the congregation and clergy exchange a greeting in the name of Christ.

Psalter / psalm—The hymnbook of the people of Israel / the individual psalms as poetic reflections on God and the relationship of God with humankind.

rite / ritual—The form of a liturgy.

rubrics—Directions give in the BCP, typically printed in italics.

sacristy—A room in which clergy dress and prepare for a liturgy.

sexton—A person responsible for the physical care and custody of a church property.

stole—A narrow band of fabric worn around the neck, or over the shoulder, by a cleric as a sign of office.

vestry room—A part of the church building or adjacent structure used for meetings.